ORDINANCES

AND

BY-LAWS

OF THE

CITY OF DETROIT

REVISED AND PUBLISHED BY ORDER OF

THE COMMON COUNCIL.

DETROIT:
WILBUR F. STOREY, PRINTER TO THE CITY.
1859.

REVISED ORDINANCES

AND

BY-LAWS OF THE CITY OF DETROIT.

Be it ordained by the Common Council of the City of Detroit.

TITLE ONE.

OF THE CITY OFFICERS.

CHAPTER I.

To Define the Powers and Duties of City Attorney.

SECTION 1. The City Attorney shall have the charge of, and conduct all, the law business of the Corporation, and of all the Boards, Officers, Departments, and Committees thereof, and all other law business in which the City shall be interested, when so ordered by the Common Council, and shall draw all leases, deeds, contracts, and ordinances of the City. Powers and duties of

SEC. 2. He shall keep his office in such place as may be designated and provided by the City, and shall execute bonds to the Corporation in the amount of two thousand dollars. Office.

SEC. 3. He shall, in writing, advise the Common Council, all Boards of the City, and their Officers and Committees, respectively, and the chief officer of any department or bureau of the city government, upon all matters which may be submitted to him for his opinion. Advise Council & officers.

SEC. 4. He shall certify to the correctness of the form of all official bonds, deeds, leases, and contracts of any kind, in which the City Certify to bonds, &c.

TITLE I. CHAPTER 1.

is interested, before the same shall be accepted or adopted by the Common Council or any officer of the Corporation.

SEC. 5. He shall, when required by the Common Council, prepare the draft of any bill to be presented by the Corporation of the City to the Legislature for passage, with a proper memorial.

Prosecute & defend act'ns for & against city.

SEC. 6. He shall prosecute and defend all actions which may be brought by or against the Corporation, or any board or officer thereof.

SEC. 7. He shall institute actions against all persons owing the Corporation for rents and licenses, or whn may have incurred any penalty or forfeiture under the charter and ordinances, or by reason of the breach of the condition of any official bond.

File statement.

SEC. 8. He shall, once in every quarter, file a written statement, under oath, with the Controller, stating the nature and amount of any debt due to the Corporation, recovered by him, the person against whom, and the tribunal before which, it was recovered, and the time when he recovered the same; and he shall, at the time of making said statement, pay all sums so recovered to the City Treasurer, who shall give him a voucher therefor, a copy of which he shall file with the Controller.

Report when made.

SEC. 9. He shall, on the first Tuesday in January in each year, report to the Common Council the titles and nature of all actions prosecuted or defended by him during the preceding year, and what actions are pending, what determined, and how, and such other informationg concernin the law business of the City, as he deems proper.

To keep register.

SEC. 10. He shall keep in proper books, to be provided for the purpose, a register of all actions prosecuted or defended by him, and of all proceedings had therein; a list of all contracts, bonds, and other papers certified to by him, and copies of all opinions which he shall give upon any point submitted to him.

Disbursements, statement of.

SEC. 11. He shall, at the expiration of every three months, during his term of office, furnish the Controller with a sworn statement of all the disbursements which he may have made in conducting the law business of the City, for the amount of which the Controller shall draw his warrant upon the Treasurer.

Additional counsel.

SEC. 12. He shall, when he deems it necessary, in the trial or argument of causes of importance, in which the City may be a party, or interested, request such additional counsel or aid as he may designate: *Provided*, that he shall, in all cases, inform the Common

Council whom he wishes to employ, and shall employ no one without their consent.

SEC. 13. He shall, without special direction from the Common Council, institute all actions for rents,, penalties, forfeitures, and license moneys, for all trespasses and injuries upon and to the property of the City, or any Board thereof. To com'ence actions.

SEC. 14. He shall examine all tax and assessment rolls before their confirmation, and make such alterations in the form thereof as may be necessary to their legality. Tax, &c. rolls to examine.

SEC. 15. All the principal officers of the City shall, from time to time, place in the hands of the attorney, for his action, all claims for debt, money, or damages done to the City, which may arise in, or grow out of, the office and business under their charge; and whenever suit is commenced against the Corporation, the officer on whom process is served shall deliver the same to him. To receive claims from officers.

CHAPTER II.

Relative to Collectors.

SECTION 1. The Collectors of the several wards of the city of Detroit shall colect the city tax within the bounds of their respective wards, and shall be entitled to such rate per cent. for compensation as the Common Council may from time to time by resolution prescribe: *Provided always,* That the said compensation shall not exceed five per cent., and that when the Common Council have neglected to fix another and lower rate of per cent. before the tax rolls are put into the hands of the said Collectors for collection, that then each of said Collectors shall be entitled to receive the said sum of five per cent. on the amount collected by him. Shall collect tax in several wards, compensation.

SEC. 2. The penalty of the bonds of each Collector, given to said city for the faithful performance of his duty, shall be in a sum at least double the amount of the taxes of the preceding year, in the ward for which said Collector has been elected or re-appointed, and in such further and other sum as the Common Council may by resolution direct. Amount of bonds.

SEC. 3. In addition to the condition prescribed for official bonds by the charter of said city, the bond of each Collector shall be con- Conditions.

ditioned that he shall account for the total amount of taxes charged to him and put into his hands for collection, in accordance with the ordinances, by the City Treasurer of said city.

Duties of Collectors.

SEC. 4. It shall be the duty of each Collector, during the time he has any tax roll in his hands for collection, at least once in every seven days, to deposit with the City Treasurer of said city all sums of money collected by him during said days and since his last deposit, for which sums he shall take the Treasurer's receipt, which he shall, within twenty-four hours after receiving the same, show to the Controller of said city, and shall, at the same time, file with said Controller a statement in writing that the amount so deposited by him with said Treasurer was all the money belonging to the Corporation of said city, collected by him and in his possession at the time of making said deposit, which statement shall be signed by the Collector making the same, and sworn to by him before the Controller, who shall report said statement to the Common Council, with his allowance or disallowance endorsed thereon, in the same manner as other accounts audited and endorsed by him. But in case any Collector shall not have collected any money during said seven days, then he shall report the fact to the Treasurer, and shall make a sworn statement of the same to the Controller; and if once at least in every seven days said Collector shall not make a deposit with the Treasurer, and make either the first or last of the statements or the report herein required to be made, he shall, upon conviction, be punished by not more than six months' imprisonment, or by a fine not to exceed two hundred dollars, or by both said fine and imprisonment, in the discretion of the Court.

Duties of Controller & Treasurer in case of non-compliance of Collectors.

SEC. 5. If any Collector shall fail to comply with any of the provisions of the preceding section, it shall be the duty of the Controller and Treasurer, or either of them having knowledge of the fact, to report such failure to the Common Council, and also to notify the City Attorney of the same, and said Attorney shall complain of and prosecute in the Recorder's Court, the Collector so reported, and shall, if said Collector shall allow a period of fourteen days to pass, without complying with the provisions of this ordinance, bring suit against said Collector and his sureties upon his official bonds.

Shall apply to City Collector.

SEC. 6. The provisions of this ordinance shall also apply to the City Collector.

SEC. 7. Chapter four of the Revised Ordinances of the year 1855, is hereby repealed.

SEC. 8. This ordinance shall go into force five days after its passage.

CHAPTER III.

To Punish Persons Resisting Collectors in the Performance of their Duties.

City & ward collectors empowered to levy and sell under warrant.

SECTION 1. That any person or persons who shall resist, obstruct, or hinder any City Collector or Ward Collector of said city in levying upon or taking into possession any goods and chattels under and by virtue of a warrant, legally issued and directed to said City Collector or Ward Collector, for the collection of any tax or assessment of said city—said goods and chattels being legally liable to be so levied on and taken into possession by said City Collector or Ward Collector—shall be punished by a fine not to exceed five hundred dollars, or by imprisonment not to exceed one year, or by both such fine and imprisonment, in the discretion of the Court.

Penalty for resisting.

SEC. 2. Any person who shall prevent any City Collector or Ward Collector from entering upon any house or premises occupied by him or her, for the purpose of searching for or levying on goods and chattels, under any warrant legally issued for the collection of tax or assessment, which the person so occupying said house or premises is liable to pay, shall be punished by the same fine or imprisonment, or by both, in the discretion of the Court, as is provided in the preceding section.

SEC. 3. This ordinance shall take effect on and after its passage.

CHAPTER IV.

To Define the Powers and Duties of Street Commissioners.

Districts.

SECTION 1. The city of Detroit shall be divided into two districts, to be respectively called the Western Street Commissioner's District and the Eastern Street Commissioner's District, in and for each of which districts a Street Commissioner shall be appointed.

TITLE I. CHAPTER 4.

First and second districts. SEC. 2. The First Street Commissioner's District shall comprise all that portion of said city lying and being west of the west line of Woodward avenue in said city. The Second Street Commissioner's District shall include said Woodward Avenue and all the territory of said city east thereof.

Duties of Commis'oner SEC. 3. The Street Commissioner for each District shall superintend the construction, pavement, repair, and cleaning of side-walks, cross-walks, streets, lanes, alleys, public places, culverts and bridges, within his District.

Office. SEC. 4. He shall keep his office in such place as shall be provided by the City, in which he shall file and preserve copies of all bills for work certified by him as hereinafter directed, of all resolutions of the Common Council, directed to him, of all opinions given to him by the City Attorney, and of all orders given by any officer of the City, having authority to issue orders to him.

To keep a Journal. SEC. 5. He shall also keep in a book or books, to be provided by the City, a journal of all his official acts, the names of all persons working under him, the nature and time of their employment, and their compensation, and a correct and business-like account of all the expenses of his offices.

To present an acc. of expenditures. SEC. 6. He shall, once in each week, draw and present to the Controller an accurate account of all the expenses for work done in his District during that week, (except work being performed under contract,) and in said account shall state the name of each man in his employ, the character of work performed by him, the exact number of days or half days which each man has actually worked, his wages per day, and the total amount due to him, which account shall be certified to by him, and shall be audited by the Controller, like all other accounts: Proviso. *Provided always*, That the amounts to which each man is entitled to by said account shall, after being so audited, be paid in no case to the Commissioner certifying the account, but to the person who is entitled thereto.

Make purchases in name of city. SEC. 7. In all cases where, by the order of the Common Council, or in the course of his duties, a Street Commissioner shall be obliged to purchase any materials or goods of any kind to be used in his District, he shall purchase the same in the name of the city, and the account for said materials or goods, certified by him, shall be audited by the Controller, and paid to the person furnishing said goods and materials.

SEC. 8. Street Commissioners shall, in no case, make a profit upon any work performed, or material furnished, by them; nor shall they certify to any bill containing charges for more than the actual cost of the work or material for which said bill is rendered. To certify to actual cost of work, &c.

SEC. 9. The Street Commissioner of each District shall, on the first Tuesday of January in each year, render a report to the Common Council of the operations of his office during the preceding year, in which report he shall give the names of employees, the wages received by them, the nature and expense of every operation carried on under his control, and such other information or suggestions as he may deem proper, so that said report shall fully embrace and explain all that he has done officially during said year, and the expenses of his District for that year. He shall also furnish to the Controller, or Committee on Ways and Means, such information as they may demand, relative to the expenses of his District. Report to C. Council in Jan. of each year.

SEC. 10. It shall be the duty of each Street Commissioner, from time to time, to report to the Common Council the condition of streets within his District, to supervise the labor, and report the misconduct or negligence of Overseers of Highways within his District, and to report to the City Marshal all breaches of the laws and ordinances relative to the streets and public highways occurring within the same. To report condition of streets, and all negligences.

CHAPTER V.

Relative to City Surveyor.

SECTION 1. It shall be the duty of the City Surveyor, when so directed by the Common Council, to ascertain and establish the proper grade to any avenue, street, lane, alley or sidewalk within the limits of said city, and when required, to run out and stake off the same. Shall establish the grade of streets, &c.

SEC. 2. It shall also be his duty to make all necessary surveys, and superintend the construction, enlargement, or alteration of all drains connecting with the main or lateral sewers of said city, and shall record the same in a book to be provided by said Common Council, and deposit the same with the City Clerk at the termination of his said office. Shall survey and superintend the construction or alteration of drains.

SEC. 3. He shall also make all necessary surveys, and give such information as may be needed by any committee, or by the Superin- Shall make surveys and give informa-

TITLE I. CHAPTER 5.

tion to the Superintendent of Hydraulics, and shall consult and act with committees of requiring official information from him.

tendent of the Water Works, in laying down, extending or connecting the water logs or pipes of said water works in said city, and shall at all times, when required, consult and act with any standing or special committee, who may desire any information or assistance in any matter or thing connected with the duties of his office where the city of Detroit is concerned.

Shall deliver books and papers to City Clerk, and when required report to the Council.

SEC. 4. He shall also deliver over to the City Clerk all papers, plans and drafts relating to any survey made by order of the Common Council, and shall also make a written report of his doings and proceedings in all cases when required so to do by the Common Council.

Salary of

SEC. 5. The salary allowed by said Council to the City Surveyor shall be in full for all services rendered and shall also be in full for all incidental, as well as other labor performed by him as said Surveyor, or by any of his assistants.

CHAPTER VI.

Relative to City Historiographer.

Duties of

SECTION 1. There shall be appointed by the Common Council, an officer to be called the Historiographer, who shall hold his office during the pleasure of the Council.

To collect and keep all books, papers, &c., connected with the History of the City of Detroit.

SEC. 2. It shall be the duty of the Historiographer to collect together, receive and safely keep all such books, papers, documents, and other matters, connected with, and illustrating the history of the city of Detroit, as he may be able to procure without expense to the city.

To make a report annually of the state of his department to the Com. Council

SEC. 3. It shall be the duty of the Historiographer to report annually, (and at such other time as he shall be required to do,) to the Common Council, the state and condition of his department.

To deliver up all books, papers, &c., and penalty for default.

SEC. 4. The Historiographer shall at any time when required by the Council, deliver over to such persons as the Council may direct, all books, papers and documents, and other things that may at any time come into his possession as such officer, and in default thereof, he shall be liable to a penalty of one hundred dollars.

Office honorary.

SEC. 5. The office of Historiographer being honorary, no compensation shall be allowed to said officer.

CHAPTER VII.

Relative to City Collector and Special Assessments.

City Collector to be appointed.

SECTION 1. That there shall be appointed by the Common Council an officer to be called the City Collector, who shall hold his office during the pleasure of the Council, from and after the first day of June, in the year in which he is appointed, and until his successor is duly elected and qualified; said City Collector shall have and possess the same powers and qualifications, under the provisions of this ordinance, as the ward Collectors of said city, and take the same oath as other city officers, and before entering upon the duties of his office, give a bond to said city, with one or more securities, to be approved by the Common Council, in the sum of twenty thousand dollars, conditioned for the faithful performance of the duties of his office, and perform all the duties which the By-Laws, Ordinances, or Resolutions of the Common Council may from time to time direct or require; and on the determination of his said office, or in case he shall die during the time, or before the accounts thereof be finally closed, that he or his respective legal representatives shall well and truly settle his said accounts, and pay over to the City Treasurer the balance, which may be found to have been in his or their hands respectively, due to said corporation, and shall deliver up to the Mayor or Common Council all his books of accounts, and all official vouchers that may have come into his hands.

Bonds of

Duties of

SEC. 2. It shall be the duty of said City Collector to collect the special taxes or assessments of said city, laid or imposed by authority of the Common Council of said city. The said City Collector shall have full power and authority to collect said taxes or assessments pursuant to the laws and ordinances of said city, and he shall at least once in each week, deposit with the City Treasurer all moneys by him collected up to the time of making each deposit, and, as far as practicable, the same money collected, and report to the Common Council all his doings relative to any collections which may be entrusted to him, once in every month, or oftener if required, and every such report shall be accompanied by the affidavit of the Collector making the same, duly sworn to before the City Controller, that such report contains a true account of all moneys by him collected for said city, during the time embraced in said report.

TITLE I. CHAPTER 7.

City Controller to deliver special assessments to Treasurer, when they shall be delivered to Collector and warrant.

SEC. 3. Whenever any special tax or assessment shall hereafter be laid or imposed, by authority of the Common Council of said city, the City Controller shall cause the assessment rolls for said special tax or assessment to be delivered to the City Treasurer, who shall give a receipt for the same and be charged therewith. The Treasurer shall retain the said assessment rolls in his office for the space of twenty days from and after the date of such delivery, and during the said period, while said rolls are so retained, any person assessed therein may pay the amount of his or her tax or assessment to the City Treasurer, who shall receive the same and give a receipt therefor, and mark the same as paid upon the said rolls. Upon the expiration of the said period of twenty days, it shall be the duty of the City Treasurer to deliver the said assessment rolls, or a certified copy of the same, adding thereto the cost of printing or other costs, to the Common Council of said city, who shall issue a warrant under the seal of said city, directed to the City Collector of said city, with a command to levy and collect all sums or assessments then remaining unpaid, with the costs and charges thereon, by distress and sale of the goods and chattels of the person against whom said assessment has been made, or those who may be liable to pay the same, and further commanding the City Collector to make returns to the Common Council, within thirty days thereafter.

How Collector shall proceed.

SEC. 4. Upon receiving the assessment roll, or a copy thereof, and warrant, it shall be the duty of the City Collector to proceed to demand and collect the several sums mentioned therein, and if any person shall neglect or refuse to pay the same, then, if he can find any goods or chattels of the person liable therefor, he shall levy thereon; but before he shall proceed to sell such goods and chattels, he shall give ten days' previous notice of the time and place of sale, by causing the same to be posted up in three of the most conspicuous places in said city, and the property levied upon shall be sold at public auction to the highest bidder; and the City Collector shall render the overplus, if any, after deducting the costs and charges of such distress and sale, to the person entitled thereto. The City Collector shall, in all cases, be entitled to demand cents on the dollar on the amount of the assessment, for his services, which the person so assessed shall pay.

SEC. 5. The City Collector shall make return of his doings within the time mentioned in said warrant, to the Common Council, if in session; but if not, then at their next ensuing meeting; and in such return describe the goods and chattels sold, and the amount which each article sold for. But if goods and chattels cannot be found, or if such person or persons mentioned in said roll are non-residents of said city, the City Collector shall state such fact, verified by an affidavit taken before the City Controller, and annex the same to a list of such lands on which the assessments have not been paid. TITLE I. CHAPTER 7. Collector to make return.

SEC. 6. Said warrant may be renewed from time to time, if the Common Council shall so direct. Warrant for collection may be renewed.

SEC. 7. Upon making such return, the City Treasurer shall proceed and sell such lots in the same manner as is prescribed for city taxes. Duty of City Treasurer upon return.

SEC. 8. The following or other sufficient forms may be used in proceedings under this chapter:

Form of Warrant. Forms.

STATE OF MICHIGAN, } ss.
City of Detroit. }

To the City Collector of the City of Detroit, Greeting;

In the name of the People of the State of Michigan, you are hereby commanded that you collect from each person or set of persons named in the foregoing tax roll, or of any person liable to pay, the amount of money set opposite his, her or their names, respectively, and on the refusal or neglect of any such person to pay said tax, costs and charges thereon, including   per cent. for your services, that you then levy the same by distress and sale of the goods and chattels of such person, according to law, and that you have said roll and this warrant and the receipt of the Treasurer of said city for the amount by you collected, before the Common Council of said city, within thirty days from the date hereof—and fail not, at your peril.

In testimony whereof, I have hereunto set my hand, and caused [L. S.] the seal of said city to be affixed at the city of Detroit aforesaid, this   day of   A. D. 18

Controller.

TITLE I. CHAPTER 7.

Notice of Sale of Property.

STATE OF MICHIGAN, } ss.
City of Detroit, }

Notice is hereby oiven, that, pursuant to law in such case made and provided, there will be sold at public auction, to the highest bidder, at in the city of Detroit, at o'clock in the noon of day of A. D. 18 , the following goods and chattels, viz.: [here description] or so much thereof as may be necessary to satisfy the amount of a certain assessment made by the Common Council of the city of Detroit, against for defraying the expenses of , together with the legal costs and charges which have accrued in the premises.

By order of the Common Council,

———, City Collector of said city.

Dated at the city of Detroit, }
this day of A. D 18 . }

Return on City Collector's Warrant.

STATE OF MICHIGAN, } ss.
City of Detroit. }

To the Hon. the Common Council of said City:

The undersigned begs leave to submit the following list of lands of residents, (or non-residents,) which were taxed for (here set forth the object for which the tax was laid) on the day of A. D. 18 , according to the assessment roll to me heretofore delivered, but which I have not been able to collect.

[Here copy the assessment roll, so far as it relates to unpaid assessments.]

Given at the city of Detroit, }
this day of A. D. 18 . }

[Let an affidavit of the following form be added:]

STATE OF MICHIGAN, } ss.
City of Detroit. }

City Collector of said city, being duly sworn, saith that the foregoing return contains the description of all lands, and the names of all persons taxed on the assessment roll of the day of A. D. 18 , and that the several sums mentioned in the foregoing list, remain due and unpaid, and that he has not, upon diligent enquiry, been able to find or discover any goods or chattels belonging to, or in the possession of the persons charged with or liable to pay the said assessment, whereon to levy the same; and this deponent further saith, that the persons mentioned in said list as non-residents are, as he believes, non-residents.

————City Collector of said city.

Subscribed and sworn to, this day of A. D. 18 before me, City Controller of said city.

CHAPTER VIII.

Relative to Chimney Sweeps.

SECTION 1. There shall be nominated by the Board of Fire Wardens of the city of Detroit, subject to the approval of the Common Council, one Chimney Sweeper for the city, who shall have full power to appoint others under him, according to the subsequent provisions of this chapter. How appointed.

SEC. 2. No person shall hereafter follow the business or occupation of a Chimney Sweeper, either by himself, or others, within the city of Detroit, unless he shall have been approved in the manner prescribed in section one, and shall give bonds to the city of Detroit, in the penal sum of fifty dollars, conditioned for the faithful performance of his duties according to the provisions hereinafter contained, and shall have registered his name and the names of all persons employed by him as assistants, with a number affixed to every such name, in a book to be kept by the City Clerk, and shall have obtained from said Clerk a certificate of every such registry. containing the name of the person and the number affixed in said registry, under a penalty of five dollars for every day he shall follow by himself or others the said business; and the said Clerk is hereby required to make out and deliver to the person so appointed such certificates, for each of which he shall be entitled to demand and receive one dollar. To give bonds and register their names with Clerk, and Clerk to give them certificates.

SEC. 3. Every person following the aforesaid business within said city, shall wear, and cause to be worn by the persons employed by him, on the front of their caps or hats, in full view, the same figures and numbers respectively as shall be so as aforesaid entered in the said book, and contained in his or their respective certificates, in large figures not less than two inches in length, to be made of durable tin or copper, with the word "Sweep," legibly painted on said badge. To wear a badge and penalty for default.

Every person who shall violate the provisions of this section shall forfeit one dollar.

Duty of.

SEC. 4. Every such Chimney Sweep so appointed, who shall not within forty-eight hours after application to him, made by any inhabitant of the district to which he belongs, sweep, or cause to be swept, such chimney or chimneys as he shall be required to sweep, shall for every such offence forfeit and pay the sum of three dollars.

Fees of.

SEC. 5. Each Chimney Sweeper so appointed shall be entitled to demand and receive for every chimney so swept, the following sums and no more, to wit:—for each chimney with a single flue, the sum of one shilling for every story through which said flue shall pass, and six cents for each additional flue, the same to be paid by the persons respectively owning the same.

Penalty on persons whose chimneys being unswept, take fire.

SEC. 6. If any chimney in this city shall take fire and blaze out at the top, (the same not having been swept within three months next before the time of taking fire,) the occupant of such premises shall forfeit and pay the sum of one dollar and costs. But if the same shall have been swept within three months, then the person having swept the same shall forfeit and pay one dollar and costs.

CHAPTER IX.

To Prohibit and Prevent Nuisances, and to provide for the Abatement and Removal thereof.

Nuisances prohibited within the city.

SECTION 1. No person or persons shall permit on his, her, or their premises, within the boundaries of said city, or within a half a mile therefrom, of which he, or she, or they may be the occupant or occupants, agent or agents, having charge thereof, the exercise of any unwholesome or offensive trade or calling, to suffer any building, sewer, or other thing whatsoever to remain on said premises until in any manner they shall become offensive, hurtful, dangerous or unwholesome to the neighborhood or travelers; and it shall be the duty of the officers and members of the Board of Health, or of the City Marshal, or Street Commissioner of said city, to whom complaint of the condition of said premises is made, or to whose knowledge their condition shall in any manner come, to give notice to said occupant

Marshal and S't Comm'r to notify owner or occupant to abate same.

or occupants, agent or agents, to abate any and every nuisance upon said premises, and to put said premises into a cleanly and wholesome condition within twenty-four hours after receipt of said notice; and if any person shall refuse to comply with said notice, said person shall be punished by a fine not to exceed one hundred dollars, or by not more than ninety days' imprisonment, or by both, in the discretion of the Court: and each day after the expiration of the said twenty-four hours in which said person shall neglect or refuse to comply with the exigency of said notice, shall be deemed a separate and further violation of the provisions of this section.

Penalty for neglect.

SEC. 2. If, after the expiration of said twenty-four hours, said person shall not have complied with the terms of said notice, it shall be lawful for the Board of Health, or any officer thereof, or for the Mayor, or Common Council of said city, to order the City Marshal, or any Street Commissioner of said city, to proceed to put said premises in a cleanly and wholesome condition by removing any putrefaction, or any stinking, unhealthy, or decayed substance, dung, provisions, vegetables, or other matter or thing whatever which is offensive, or dangerous, or detrimental to health, or which may be forbidden by the ordinances of said city, and to report the same to the City Attorney, whose duty it shall be to bring suit in the name of the city against the occupant or occupants, agent or agents, having charge of said premises, for the costs and charges incurred by said Board of Health, or any other officer mentioned in this section, in pursuance of the duties herein enjoined upon them; and if any person shall resist, obstruct, or hinder said Board of Health, or any other officer, in the performance of a duty under this section, said person shall be punished by a fine not to exceed five hundred dollars, or by not more than one year's imprisonment.

Board of Health, Mayor and C. Council may order the Marshal & S't Com'r to abate the same.

City Att'y to sue for costs of abatement of nuisance.

SEC. 3. Whenever, in order to abate any nuisance, the Common Council of said city shall deem it necessary to fill up, level, or drain any lot or premises therein, it shall be the duty of the City Surveyor to survey said premises and estimate the cost and expense of such filling up, leveling, or drainage, and to make out an assessment roll in which said costs and expenses shall be assessed upon the said lot or premises, which roll shall be reported by him to the said Council, and shall be made, confirmed, and collected, and be a lien on said lot or premises in all respects as other special assessments are; and as soon

City Surv'or to estimate cost to abate nuisance when order'd by Council.

Lien.

as said roll is confirmed it shall be the duty of the Street Commissioner of the district in which said lot or premises are situated, without further order from the said Council, to cause said lot or premises to be filled up, leveled, or drained, in the manner declared necessary by said Common Council.

Limits within which putrid substances are not to be deposited.

SEC. 4. No person shall bury, deposit, or leave within the limits of said city, or within one mile distant therefrom, or keep or have on the premises owned or occupied by him or her in said city, any dead carcass, putrid or unsound beef, pork, fish, hides, skins, and any article, substance, or thing that is unwholesome or nauseous; and any person violating the provisions of this section shall be punished by a fine not to exceed one hundred dollars, or by imprisonment not to exceed ninety days.

Penalty.

SEC. 5. No person shall cast, leave, or keep in or adjoining any street, lane, avenue, alley, public place, or square, or in any yard, lot, field, or premises in said city, any bones, putrid, unsound, unwholesome, or refuse meat or beef of any animal, whether salted or otherwise, or any unsound pork, fish, hides, skins, vegetables, horns, or the whole or part of any carcass, or any stinking or rotten soap-grease, tallow, or other substance, or the offals, garbage, or other offensive or useless parts of any beeves, calves, sheep, hogs, or other cattle; and any person violating the provisions of this section shall be punished by a fine not to exceed one hundred dollars, or by imprisonment not to exceed ninety days.

Not to be deposited on docks or thrown into the river.

SEC. 6. No person shall place, deposit, or keep in any dock or wharf, within the limits of said city, any straw, hay, or green boughs, manure, cord wood, vegetables, or any perishable materials, any human excrement, animal carcass, bones, horns, shells, meat, hides, offals, garbage, or any unwholesome or decayed matter or thing; no person shall cast or deposit in the waters of the Detroit river, within the limits of said city, any such straw, hay, boughs, manure, cord wood, vegetables, perishable materials, human excrement, animal carcass, bones, horns, shells, meat, hides, offals, garbage, or unwholesome or decayed matter or thing; and any person violating the provisions of this section shall be punished by a fine not to exceed one hundred dollars, or by imprisonment not to exceed ninety days.

Nuisances not to run into streets, alleys, &c.

SEC. 7. No person shall cast or throw, or suffer to run into any street, lane, or alley of said city, from his or her house, lot, or premises, into and upon any adjoining house, lot, or premises, any stinking, noxious, impure, offensive, or unwholesome water, or substance or thing in a liquid or flowing state; and any person violating the provisions of this section shall be punished by a fine not to exceed one hundred dollars, or by imprisonment not to exceed ninety days.

Brewers, distillers, &c., not allowed to suffer the water, &c., to run on surface.

SEC. 8. No brewer, distiller, dyer, soap maker, hat maker, tanner, or other person shall cast or throw, or suffer the water from his manufactory, house, store, or establishment, to run into and upon the surface of any street, lane, alley, or public place, or into and upon any adjoining lot or premises; and any person violating the provisions of this section shall be punished by a fine not to exceed one hundred dollars, or by not more than ninety days' imprisonment.

Ashes, offal, &c., not to be thrown in streets or alleys.

SEC. 9. No person shall throw, cast, or lay any ashes, offal, vegetables, garbage, dross, cinders, shells, straw, shavings, dirt, or rubbish of any kind, in any street, lane, or alley of said city; and any person violating the provisions of this section shall be punished by a fine not to exceed one hundred dollars, or by not more than ninety days' imprisonment.

Butchers to cause their slaughter houses cleansed daily.

SEC. 10. Every butcher, or other person occupying any slaughter house in said city, shall, on every day on which any animal shall be killed therein, between the first day of June and the first day of November in each year, cause the house to be thoroughly washed and cleansed; any person violating the provisions of this section shall be punished by a fine not to exceed fifty dollars, or by not more than ninety days' imprisonment.

Removal of offals, &c.

SEC. 11. Every butcher or other person, immediately after killing any animal, shall destroy the offals, garbage, and other offensive or useless parts thereof, or shall cause the same to be conveyed to the place designated by the Common Council for receiving such noxious and offensive matters and things as are within the province of the City Scavenger; and any person violating the provisions of this section shall be punished by a fine not to exceed one hundred dollars, or by not more than ninety days' imprisonment.

Carts, &c., used in removing offal, &c., not to stand in alleys, streets, &c., in city.

SEC. 12. No cart, wagon, or other vehicle, in or upon which there shall be a box, hogshead, barrel, cask, or other vessel used or intended to be used for the purpose of containing or conveying swill, offals, garbage, or excrement, shall, when not in actual use, stand in any street, lane, or alley of said city; and any person violating the pro-

TITLE I. CHAPTER 9.

visions of this section, shall, upon conviction thereof, be punished by a fine not to exceed fifty dollars, or by not more than forty days' imprisonment.

Casks so used to be tight and covered.

SEC. 13. Said box, hogshead, barrel, cask, or other vessels used, or intended to be used for the purpose aforesaid, shall be perfectly tight, and covered, so as to prevent the contents thereof from leaking or spilling; and any person violating the provisions of this section shall be punished by a fine not to exceed ten dollars, or by not more than five days' imprisonment.

Scavengers not to spill any nuisance on ground.

SEC. 14. No Scavenger shall suffer or permit any excrement or other disgusting and offensive thing, being conveyed by him through the streets of said city, to be dropped or spilled upon the ground; and any person violating the provisions of this section shall be punished by a fine not to exceed fifty dollars, or by not more than forty days' imprisonment.

Mayor to license scavengers.

SEC. 15. The Mayor of said city may, from time to time, license any trustworthy persons to be Scavengers of said city, upon their filing proper security for the performance of their duties, and paying to the City Treasurer the sum of one dollar for their licenses; and any person who shall follow the business of a Scavenger for hire in said city, unless so licensed, shall be punished by a fine not to exceed fifty dollars, or by not more than forty days' imprisonment.

City Clerk to register the names of scavengers.

SEC. 16. The Mayor shall transmit to the City Clerk the names of all persons so licensed by him, and said Clerk shall register said name with the date of the license.

Rights of persons so licensed.

SEC. 17. The persons licensed as Scavengers aforesaid, shell exclusively enjoy the right, and possess and receive emoluments, to clean privies within said city; and shall, under the direction of the Marshal, or any Street Commissioner of said city, have lawful authority to enter, unmolested and unhindered, any lot or premises in said city on which there shall be any privy or backhouse, and to examine said privy or backhouse, and the same when filled with excrement to a level with the surface of the ground or lot on which they stand, between the hours of ten o'clock in the evening and four o'clock in the morning, to cleanse and empty them of their contents, and such contents to remove to a place or places designated by the Common Council of said city; and if said Scavenger, or any of them, remove said

When work to be done.

contents to any other place, they or he shall be punished by a fine of twenty dollars, or by fifteen days' imprisonment for each offence.

Scavengers to clean privies when requested.

SEC. 18. Said Scavenger shall, when requested by any person to clean any privy within said city, clean the same at the cost of the person requesting the same to be done, in the same manner, and remove the contents thereof to the same place provided in the preceding section.

Duties of owners.

SEC. 19. It shall be the duty of each and every owner or occupier of a privy within said city, whenever his or her privy is filled with excrement within a foot of the surface of the ground or lot on which it is situated, to cause said privy to be cleansed forthwith by the City Scavenger; any person violating the provisions of the preceding section shall be punished by a fine not to exceed twenty-five dollars, or by not more than ten days' imprisonment.

To notify Marshal.

SEC. 20. All persons desiring the services of a Scavenger, under the preceding section, shall leave a written notice to that effect, stating the place where, and the person by whom, his services are needed, with the City Marshal.

Fees.

SEC. 21. Each Scavenger shall be entitled to demand and receive the sum of eight cents for each cubic foot of the contents of any privy cleaned by him, and no more.

Penalty for refusing to pay fees.

SEC. 22. If any person or persons whose privy or privies have been cleaned by any Scavenger without request, under the provisions of this ordinance, shall refuse or neglect to pay said Scavenger his lawful charges for cleaning the same, said person or persons shall, upon conviction thereof, be fined a sum sufficient to pay said charges and the costs of prosecution.

Penalty for neglect of duty when ordered by Marshal.

SEC. 23. If any Scavenger, licensed under this ordinance, shall refuse or neglect to clean any privy within the city of Detroit, within forty-eight hours after he is notified so to do by the City Marshal, or when he shall know the same to be full, or shall deposit the contents of any privy cleaned by him in any place other than the place prescribed by the Common Council of said city, or shall discharge any of his duties in a careless or improper manner, or neglect to repair any damage to the fences, buildings, and grounds of any person, made by him in the discharge of his duties, or shall demand any higher price than that fixed by this ordinance for his services, or if he shall neglect to clean the dirt occasioned by him in cleaning any

TITLE I. CHAPTER 9.

privy, or dropped by him from any cart, vessel, or vehicle, in removing the contents of any privy, he shall be punished by a fine not to exceed fifty dollars, or by not more than thirty days' imprisonment.

Scavenger to remove dead animals when order'd

SEC. 24. It shall be the duty of any Scavenger, when ordered by the Board of Health, any officer or member thereof, by any Street Commissioner, or the City Marshal, to remove within twenty-four hours, to a place to be designated for that purpose by the Common Council, any carcass of any animal found and being in any of the streets, alleys, or public places of said city; and he shall receive for removing said carcass, such sum of money as the Common Council may prescribe; and if said Scavenger refuses or neglects so to remove said carcass, or removes it to any place other than that so designated, he shall be punished by a fine not to exceed fifty dollars, or by not more than twenty-five days' imprisonment.

Compensat'n

Scavengers not to clean privies when forbidden.

SEC. 25. Whenever, at any season of the year, the Common Council, or the Board of Health of said city, shall declare it unwholesome to clean any privy in said city, if any Scavenger or other person shall clean any privy at said season, or during the time designated by said Common Council, or Board of Health, said Scavenger or person shall be punished by a fine of ten dollars, or by imprisonment for ten days.

All cesspools to be of brick

SEC. 26. No sink, privy, or cesspool shall be constructed in any part of the said city, unless the same shall be constructed of brick or stone, and shall be sunk at least four feet from the surface of the earth, where that depth is practicable and consistent with proper drainage into some public sewer or drain. No person shall drain his or her premises, or any cellar, privy, or sink, into any other place than some public sewer or drain of said city: *Provided*, That there is a public sewer within one hundred feet of said premises, cellar, or sink. No person shall enclose or cover any sink, privy, or cesspool, or arch over, or place upon the same any covering whatever, until said privy, sink, or cesspool shall have been examined by some member of the Board of Health, or by the Street Commissioner of the district in which said privy, sink, or cesspool is situated; and any person violating any provisions of this section shall be punished by a fine not to exceed thirty dollars, or by not more than ten days' imprisonment.

To enter public sewers or drains.

Proviso.

SEC. 27. The owner of any sink, or cesspool, or the person occupying the premises on which the same are, shall not permit the contents thereof to rise to a greater height than within a foot of the surface of the ground; and any person who shall violate the provisions of this section shall be punished by a fine not to exceed fifty dollars, or by not more than thirty days' imprisonment.

Height beyond which the contents of cesspools are not to rise

SEC. 28. No person shall clean any sink, orcess pool, or any drain connected therewith, or with any privy, save during the hours of ten o'clock in the evening and four o'clock in the morning, and said person shall, during that time, and on the same night, cause the contents thereof to be removed by a City Scavenger, and shall pay said Scavenger for his services in removing said contents the sum of six cents per cubic foot, for each and every foot of the solid contents so removed; and any person violating the provisions of this section shall be punished by a fine not to exceed twenty dollars, or by not more than ten days' imprisonment.

Time when privies, &c., to be cleans'd

SEC. 29. No person shall throw or deposit any carrion, carcass of any animal, any vegetable substance, garbage, or offals of fish, poultry, or of any animal, into any sink, privy, cesspool, drain, or sewer, in said city; and any person violating the provisions of this section shall be punished by a fine not to exceed twenty-five dollars, or by fifteen days' imprisonment.

Carrion, &c., not to be thrown into sinks.

SEC. 30. No person shall use and maintain in any necessary house or privy within said city, any tub, box, cask, barrel, half barrel, or cask, in the place and stead of a vault; and any person violating the provisions of this section shall be punished by a fine not to exceed twenty-five dollars, or by fifteen days' imprisonment.

Tubs, &c., not to be used as vaults.

SEC. 31. Chapters twelve, forty, and forty-two of the Revised Ordinances of the year 1855, are hereby repealed.

Chaps. 12, 40, and 42, R. S. 1855, repeal'd

TITLE TWO.

OF TAXES AND ASSESSMENTS.

CHAPTER X.

Relative to the Assessment and Collection of City Taxes.

Duty of Attorney relative to general assessment

SECTION 1. It shall be the duty of the City Attorney to meet with the Assessors, and give them all necessary advice relative to the manner of making the general assessment, and if any property belonging to the corporation should be assessed, to request that the same should be stricken from the roll.

Proclamation for public meeting to authorize tax to be published by the.

SEC. 2. That whenever it shall be necessary to call a meeting of the freemen of said city, for the purpose of authorizing the said Common Council to assess or lay a tax on the real and personal property within the limits of said city, the notice or proclamation for convening such meeting shall be left or filed with the City Clerk, who shall cause a copy thereof to be duly published in said city, in one of the city papers and handbills.

Proceedings of meeting to be filed and recorded.

SEC. 3. If such meeting shall authorize the Common Council to assess and levy any such tax, the Chairman, or other officer of the meeting shall certify the same to the Common Council, as soon as may be, and such authority so certified shall be recorded in the Journal, and filed by the City Clerk.

School, highway and sewer taxes to be delivered to Collectors—when.

SEC. 4. All city, school, highway, and sewer taxes or assessments not paid to City Treasurer as hereinafter provided, shall be collected by the Collector of the ward wherein the same are assessed and to be collected.

Controller cause rolls to be delivered to Treasurer, and how long Treasurer may detain the same.

SEC. 5. Hereafter, when the assessment rolls for city, school, highway, and sewer taxes or assessments are completed, the City Controller shall cause the same to be delivered to the City Treasurer, who shall give a receipt for the same, and be charged therewith. The Treasurer shall retain the said assessment rolls for city, school, highway, and sewer taxes in his office until such day as shall be designated by the Council, in each year, and during said periods, while said rolls are so detained respectively, any person assessed therein may pay the amount of their taxes or assessments to the City Treasurer, who shall receive and give a receipt therefor, and mark the same as paid upon the proper roll.

City Treasurer to procure warrant to be attached to tax rolls.

SEC. 6. When the day designated in accordance with the provisions of the preceding section shall have elapsed, the City Treasurer shall request the Controller of said city to annex to each of the rolls for city, school, highway, and sewer taxes, a warrant under his hand and the corporate seal, directed to the Collector for the ward or district in which the said rolls are to be collected, commanding him to collect all sums or assessments then remaining unpaid upon the roll, to which said warrant is annexed, of the person or persons from whom said sums or assessments are due, and if any person or persons from whom such sums or assessments are due as aforesaid, shall neglect or refuse to pay the same, or any part thereof, then that he shall levy the same by distress and sale of the goods and chattels of such person; and further, that he shall make return of his doings under said warrant upon a day to be fixed by resolution of the Common Council, which said warrant may be renewed from time to time as the said Council shall deem necessary; and the said Treasurer shall deliver the said rolls and warrants to the respective Collectors of the wards wherein the same are to be collected, giving to each Collector the roll to be collected in the ward of such Collector.

Contents of warrant.

The amount unpaid on rolls to be charged to the collectors

SEC. 7. Whenever any of said rolls are delivered, as provided in the foregoing section, the Treasurer shall charge the amount unpaid thereon to the Collector receiving the same, and shall also take the receipt of such Collector therefor.

Collectors to collect and make returns

SEC. 8. Upon receiving the said rolls, the several Collectors shall proceed to collect the amounts appearing unpaid thereon, in the manner provided by the charter and ordinances of said city, and shall proceed and make returns at the times and in the manner in said charter and ordinances prescribed.

Collectors to return taxes unpaid to the Council, &c.

SEC. 9. If any of the taxes mentioned in the tax roll of any ward or district shall remain unpaid, and the Collector for such ward or district shall not be able to collect the same, he shall report and deliver to the Common Council a list of the taxes so remaining due; and on making oath before the City Clerk, or in case of his absence, before any Justice of the Peace, that the sums mentioned in such list remain unpaid, and that he has not, upon diligent enquiry, been able to discover any goods or chattels belonging to or in possession

TITLE II. CHAPTER 10. of the persons charged with or liable to pay such sums, whereon he could levy the same, he shall be credited by the City Treasurer with the amount thereof, but not otherwise. The Collector shall also designate in such report or list, all persons named in this roll who are not residents of said city: *Provided*, The Collector may make said return to the Common Council at their meeting next ensuing the time mentioned in said warrant.

Forms. SEC. 10. The following or other sufficient forms may be used in proceeding under this chapter:

Form of Warrant.

STATE OF MICHIGAN, }
City of Detroit. } SS.

To Collector of the Ward of the City of Detroit, Greeting:

In the name of the people of the State of Michigan, You are hereby commanded, that you collect from the several persons named in the foregoingo Tax Roll, or of any person liable to pay the same, the amount of highway, sewer, school, and city taxes opposite to their names respectively, together with per cent. for your services for collecting the same; and on the neglect or refusal of any such person to pay such taxes, that you then levy the same by distress and sale of goods and chattels of such person, occupant, or lessee refusing or neglecting to pay the same according to law; and that you have said roll, and the money so collected by you, and this warrant, before the Common Council of said city, on the day of 185 .

In testimony whereof, I have hereunto set my hand, and caused [L. S.] the seal of said city to be affixed, at the city of Detroit aforesaid, this day of A. D. 18 .

——— Controller.

Attest:

——— Clerk.

Notice of the Sale of Property.

STATE OF MICHIGAN, }
City of Detroit. } SS.

Notice is hereby given, that on the day of A. D. 18 , at o'clock noon, the undersigned will sell at public auction, at (or refused) to pay the city tax imposed on him for the year 18 , and which is to be levied by said sale. TITLE II. CHAPTER 10.

Dated at Detroit, this day of A. D. 18 .

} *Collector for City of Detroit.*

Collector's Return.

STATE OF MICHIGAN, } ss.
City of Detroit. }

To the Hon. the Common Council of the said City:

The undersigned begs leave to submit the following list of the lands of residents and non-residents of said city, which were taxed for the year 18 , according to the assessment roll of said city, to me heretofore delivered to be collected according to law, but which I have not been able to collect.

Names.	Description of Lands.	Valuation.		Tax.	
		Dolls.	Cents.	Dolls	Cents.

Given at the city of Detroit, this day of A. D. 18 .

} *Collector for City of Detroit.*

STATE OF MICHIGAN, } ss.
City of Detroit. }

, Collector of in said city, being duly sworn, saith that the several sums mentioned in the annexed list of city taxes for the year remain due and unpaid, and that he has not, upon diligent enquiry, been able to find or discover in said city, any goods or chattels belonging to or in possession of the persons charged with or liable to pay the said sums of money, whereon he could levy the same; and this deponent further saith that the persons mentioned in the in said city, the following property, to wit: (here describe the property,) which I have distrained because A. B. hath neglected

TITLE II. CHAPTER 11.

said lists as non-residents are, as he believes, non-residents of said city.

Collector for City of Detroit.

Subscribed and sworn to this day of A. D. 18 , before me.

Clerk of said City.

CHAPTER XI.

Relative to the Sale of Lands for Taxes and Assessments.

When lots to be sold for taxes.

SECTION 1. Whenever the City Collector or other officer of said city, authorized to collect any tax or assessment on any lands, tenements, hereditaments, or premises in said city, or on the owners or occupants thereof, shall make due return that such tax or assessment remains due and uncollected, it shall be the duty of the City Treasurer, on behalf of the Common Council, to proceed and sell such lands, tenements, hereditaments, and premises, in the manner hereinafter prescribed.

Treasurer shall give notice of sale

SEC. 2. The Treasurer shall make out a list of all such lands, the names, if known, of the owners or occupants, the amount of the delinquent tax or assessment due thereon according to such return; and the Treasurer, on behalf of the Common Council, shall cause such list, with a notice thereto attached, to be published four weeks successively in the official newspaper of said city, requiring the owners, occupants, or lessees of such lands, tenements, hereditaments, and premises, against whom such assessments have been made, to pay the same; and further notifying them, that if default shall be made in any such payment, such real estate will be sold at public auction, at a day and place therein to be specified, for the lowest term of years at which any person will offer to take the same, in consideration of advancing the sum assessed or taxed on the same, with the costs and charges in the premises.

Lots to be sold if taxes not paid.

SEC. 3. If, notwithstanding such notice, the owner or owners, occupant or occupants, lessee or lessees, or person or persons liable to pay such tax, shall neglect or refuse to pay the same with the cost and charges thereon, then the Treasurer, on behalf of the Common Council, at the place and on the day mentioned in such notice, shall commence the sale of such lands, and shall continue the same from day to day, (Sundays excepted,) until the same be sold for a term of years, for the purpose and in the manner already above expressed; but each lot or parcel of a lot owned by any one person or set of persons, against whom such assessment has been made, shall be sold by itself.

Treasurer to report sale to Common Council when purchaser entitled to conveyances and on what terms.

SEC. 4. At the close of the sale, the Treasurer shall report to the Common Council the terms for which each lot was sold, the amount bid therefor, and the name of the purchaser; and if there be no sufficient objection, the several purchasers shall be entitled to the necessary conveyances of said premises, when the time of redemption fixed by law shall have fully expired, upon paying for the expense of such conveyance the further sum of fifty cents, unless such lot shall have been sooner redeemed, in which case the purchaser shall be entitled to receive the purchase money and interest.

Treasurer to report to Council neglect of purchasers to pay.

SEC. 5. The purchasers at such sale shall pay the amount of their respective bids to the Treasurer within forty-eight hours after the sale, and if they shall neglect or refuse to pay the same within that time, the Treasurer shall report the names of such persons to the Common Council, who may elect to take the lots bid off by such purchaser.

Controller to prepare conveyance.

SEC. 6. The Controller shall prepare the necessary conveyance and deliver the same under the corporate seal, and in the corporate name execute to the purchaser, his heirs or assigns, a declaration of sale of the land so sold, which shall be attested by the Clerk.

Treasurer to keep a record of land sales.

SEC. 7. The Treasurer shall keep a correct record of all land sales, showing the time when the tax or assessment was levied, and the amount therefor, the costs and charges, the time when the lands were sold, the name of the purchaser or his assignee, the term for which the same were bid off, the time when redeemed, and by whom, with such other entries as may be necessary in the premises. Any person entitled to redeem any such lot, may, within one year from the time of sale, pay the amount due thereon, including all costs and charges, to the City Treasurer, who shall give proper receipts therefor, and shall enter a note of such redemption on said record. Whenever any premises, lands, tenements, or hereditaments shall be returned

How lands so sold may be redeemed.

TITLE II. CHAPTER II. hereafter for the non-payment of any tax or assessment, interest upon the same shall be charged as follows: fifteen per cent. per annum from the date when the same shall be so returned, up to and until the date of the sale of such premises, or the payment of the amount of such tax with interest at said rate; and from and after the sale of any lands, tenements, or hereditaments, interest upon the amount for which the same shall be sold shall be computed and charged at the rate of twenty per cent. per annum, and no person shall be entitled after sale to redeem any premises sold without payment of the said interest and principal in the manner prescribed by law.

Forms. SEC. 8. The following or other sufficient forms may be used in proceedings under this chapter:

Notice of Tax Sale.

STATE OF MICHIGAN, } ss.
City of Detroit. }

Notice is hereby given, that pursuant to law, there will be sold, at the Common Council Hall, in the city of Detroit and State of Michigan, between the hours of and , in the forenoon of the day of , A. D. 18 , at public auction, the several premises hereinafter described, each parcel separately, for the lowest term of years at which any person will offer to take the same, in consideration of advancing the sum or sums which were assessed or taxed by the Common Council of said city, for the year one thousand eight hundred and (or on the day of one thousand eight hundred and to defray the expenses of paving or planking sidewalks, or otherwise, as the case may be, in front of or adjacent to the several premises; together with costs and charges in the premises;) unless the said sum or sums, with the costs and charges thereon, shall before that time be paid and satisfied, which the owners or occupants of said premises, against whom said sum or sums have been assessed, are hereby required to do. [Here insert an accurate description of the several premises, and add to the description of each, the amount assessed, the name of the individual or individuals against whom the same is assessed, and also the amount of the costs and charges, if any, up to that time.]

Names.	Description of Lots.	Amount of Tax.	Costs of Asssessment.*

Dated at the city of Detroit, this day of A. D. 18 .

By order of the Common Council,

City Treasurer.

Form of Declaration of Sale.

This indenture, made the day of in the year of our Lord one thousand eight hundred and , between the Corporation of the city of Detroit, in the State of Michigan, of the first part; and of the second part: *Whereas*, in pursuance of, and in conformity with, the provisions of the laws of said State, relative to the city of Detroit aforesaid, providing for the assessment and collection of taxes and assessments imposed and laid by the authority of the Common Council of the city of Detroit, the lot of land hereinafter described, was, on the day of in the year one thousand eight hundred and , duly sold for the payment of the assessment (or tax) imposed thereon by the Common Council for the year one thousand eight hundred and , [if it be a special tax, say after the word " Council,"—on the day of , in the year, etc., for the expense of constructing a sidewalk in front of, and adjacent to, the said lot or premises; or other special assessment, as the case may be,] to the said party of the second part, for the sum of dollars and cents, it being the amount of the taxes and costs, and charges on said lot, for the term of years which was the least term for which any person offered to take the same, in consideration of advancing the said sum of money; and the said party of the second part having advanced and paid said sum of money as required by law,

* This column is unnecessary except in cases of special assessments.

TITLE II. CHAPTER 12.

Now, therefore, this indenture witnesseth, that the said party of the first part, in pursuance of law, and in pursuance of the sale aforesaid, and also in consideration of the premises, and of the said sum of money being duly paid and advanced as aforesaid, by the said party of the first part, the receipt whereof is hereby confessed, do by these presents declare, that they demise and lease unto the said party of the second part executors, administrators, and assigns, all that said piece or parcel of land, situate in said city of Detroit, and State of Michigan, known and described as , together with all and singular, the benefits, liberties, and privileges to said premises belonging; to have and to hold the said demised premises with the appurtenances, unto the said party of the second part, executors, administrators, and assigns, for and during the full end and term above mentioned, fully to be completed and ended; (and if the above lot shall not be redeemed according to law, within one year from the day of these presents will become absolute.)

In testimeny whereof, I, Controller of said city of Detroit, and on behalf of the said parties of the first part, [L. S.] have hereunto set my hand, and caused to be affixed hereunto the corporate seal of said city at the city of Detroit, the day and year first above written.

Controller of the city of Detroit.

By ————————*Controller of said City.*

Attest:

——————, *Clerk of said City.*

CHAPTER XII.

Relative to paving Sidewalks, Avenues, or Streets, and constructing Crosswalks.

Sidewalks, crosswalks and streets to be paved or planked.

SECTION 1. That the side and crosswalks of all streets and avenues, which are or shall be graded, and all streets and avenues, shall be paved or planked with such materials as the Common Council may direct.

SEC. 2. If the owner of any lot or premises has or shall have paved or planked the street in front of his premises to the centre thereof, according to the provisions of this chapter, and shall keep the same in good repair, such premises shall be exempt, and the owner thereof shall not be liable to pay any assessments for highway labor, upon his producing satisfactory evidence to the Street Commissioner that such person has or shall have so paved or planked such streets, or paid therefor, and shall have kept the same in good repair; and no such exemption shall be allowed to any person or persons except in the manner, and on the terms and conditions above expressed.

Persons paving, &c., in front of their premises exempted from tax.

SEC. 3. The owner of all lots on streets which have been graded, and prepared for the laying down of sidewalks, under the direction of the Common Council, are hereby authorized to pave or plank in front of their lots, under the direction of such officer or committee as the Common Council may direct.

Owners may pave or plank in front of their lots.

Sidewalks.

SEC. 4. Whenever the Common Council of said city shall deem it necessary to provide funds for defraying the expenses of paving or planking any sidewalks within the limits of said city, they shall do so by assessment on the owners or occupants of the lots or premises in front or adjacent to the sidewalks paved or planked, or directed so to be; and whenever it may be necessary to provide for the expense of constructing any crosswalks in said city, the assessments for the same shall be made in accordance with the provisions of this chapter, particularly relating thereto.

How money raised for sidewalks.

SEC. 5. Whenever the said Common Council shall have paved or planked any sidewalks in said city, or shall direct the same to be paved or planked, the City Surveyor shall make an assessment on the owner or occupants of the lots or premises in front of or adjacent to said sidewalks paved or planked, or directed so to be.

Surveyor to assess expense.

SEC. 6. The said City Surveyor shall, with all due diligence, ascertain from the best evidence in his power, all the necessary facts, and shall then make out a written report or assessment roll, stating therein the names of the owners or occupants of the lots or premises in front of, or adjacent to which such sidewalks may be paved or planked, or directed so to be; describing by itself, with sufficient accuracy, each lot or portion of a lot owned by any one person or company of persons, and also the names of such owner or several owners; and when he cannot ascertain the names of any such owners or occu-

Mode of assessment.

TITLE II. CHAPTER 12.

pants, or either of them, he shall state such fact in his report, and he shall therein state who of such owners are residents of said city, and who are non-residents; and said City Surveyor shall also, in as accurate a manner as possible, ascertain, and in said report set forth the space or number of square yards or feet paved or planked, and the quantity of curbing placed, or to be placed in front of or adjacent to the lots or premises owned or occupied by any one person or set of persons, the sum of money which such person or set of persons shall be assessed at and pay for such paving or planking, and also five cents for each description, to defray the expense of making such assessment, which report the said City Surveyor shall present to said Common Council.

Contents of Surveyor's report to be presented to the Council.

Clerk to notify owners of lots assessed by public notice.

SEC. 7. The City Clerk shall then make out a notice, directed to the several persons in said report named and proposed to be assessed, notifying them that they are about to be assessed, to defray the expenses of paving or planking the sidewalks adjacent to certain premises owned or occupied by them in said city, and that a report or assessment roll made out in the premises is on file in the office of said Clerk, for inspection, and further notifying them of the time and place when the Common Council will meet and review said report or assessment, on the request of any person conceiving himself aggrieved; which said notice shall be published in some daily newspaper printed in said city, four times during ten days.

S't Comm'r to serve notice of assessment on certain persons. Contents of notice.

SEC. 8. In addition to the printed notice provided for in the last preceding section, the Street Commissioner, as soon as any such assessment shall have been made, shall forthwith serve or cause to be served upon all persons therein interested, who are residents of the city, a written or printed notice, by delivering the same to them personally, or leaving it at the party's usual place of abode or business, which said notice shall fully set forth the place where said sidewalk, paving, or planking is ordered, and that said party is allowed ten days within which to construct the same; and if completed within that time to the satisfaction of the City Surveyor, that no expense of proceedings to collect the same shall be incurred by them; and upon the expiration of said ten days, the Street Commissioner shall make a full return to the Council of his doings, under this section, and state fully whether such notices have or have not been complied with by said parties; and if from such return it appears that said sidewalks, paving, or planking have not been constructed within the ten days prescribed, by the parties notified; then the amount of such assessment, together with all costs and charges incident to the collection thereof, shall be collected by warrant issued for that purpose by the Common Council, according to the provisions of chapter ten of these ordinances, "relative to a City Collector."

Council to examine and approve assessment.

SEC. 9. The said Common Council shall, at the time and place in said section specified, or at some session thereafter, take said assessment into consideration, and if no person appears to object to said report or roll, and no good cause to the contrary appears, and an affidavit of publication of the requisite notice having been made by some one acquainted with the facts, they shall, by a written resolution to be entered on their journal, declare that they approve of said report or assessment roll: that they receive as correct the description of the premises and the names of the individuals therein contained, and that the sum which said report states to be the correct one, which each individual or set of individuals should be assessed at and pay, be the assessment, and be collected from the respective persons liable, according to law; but if any sufficient cause appears, or is shown to said Common Council, they shall review said report or roll, and make such assessment as may be just and right in the premises; and said Common Council may, if necessary, adjourn from one time to any reasonable time, for the purpose of finishing said review of said assessment.

Plank Sidewalks.

When plank walks may be laid.

SEC. 10. The Common Council may from time to time authorize that good and substantial plank sidewalks shall be laid down and constructed in any street or part of a street, whether graded or not, as hereinbefore described, and under the direction of the City Surveyor.

How plank walks constructed.

SEC. 11. Such sidewalks shall be constructed of good pine or oak plank, which shall not be less than two inches in thickness, nor more than twelve inches wide, on oak, cedar, or hemlock sleepers, not less than four inches square, to be placed not more than three feet apart, the plank to be nailed with nails not less than forty penny, with at least three in each end of each plank, and not less than two at any other bearing, and said walks shall be of the following width: On Jefferson and Woodward avenues, six feet, and on all other streets, three feet; *Provided, however*, That the Common Council may at any time direct that such sidewalk, on any street, or part thereof, be of more or less width than is hereinbefore described, and all crosswalks shall be constructed of oak plank, not less than two and one-half inches thick, and twelve inches wide, to be laid and fastened as in this section above prescribed for sidewalks; such crosswalks to be of such width as shall be ordered by the Common Council.

Assessment for plank walks, how made.

SEC. 12. When the Common Council shall direct the construction of any such plank sidewalk, the City Surveyor shall proceed and make an assessment therefor, showing the names of the owners or occupants, (residents or non-residents,) of the premises in front of which such sidewalk is required, with a description of such premises, the length and width of such walk, and the sum of money to be assessed for constructing the same; and when any such assessment shall be completed, the same shall be reported to the Common Council, and such further proceedings had as are required by sections seven, eight, and nine of this chapter.

Persons may construct their own walks.

SEC. 13. Any parties interested shall have the privilege of constructing a plank sidewalk in front of their respective premises, after the same shall have been ordered by the Council, within the time and after the same manner as is hereinbefore provided in section eight, and shall be entitled to all the rights and privileges secured by said section.

When Council to construct walks.

SEC. 14. Whenever an assessment has been duly levied, according to the provisions of this chapter, and a return of the warrant issued for the collection of the same by the City Collector, under the provisions of section eight, has been made, the Common Council shall proceed to the construction of the sidewalk as ordered, and the property of all persons whose assessments have not been paid shall be held liable for all costs, charges, and interest incurred on their behalf in the construction of said sidewalks, and may be sold for the same, as in the case of delinquent taxes.

Who liable for expense thereof.

Certain mistakes not to vitiate assessment.

SEC. 15. Whenever by mistake or otherwise, any person may be improperly designated as the owner or occupant of any lot or premises in proceedings under this chapter or any other ordinance of said city relative to taxes or assessments, the tax or assessment shall not for such cause be vitiated, but the same shall be a lien on such lot or premises, and collected as in other cases.

SEC. 16. Whenever the Common Council of said city shall deem it necessary to provide funds necessary for defraying the expenses of grading, paving, or planking any alley, avenue, or street of said city, or any portions thereof, they shall cause an assessment to be made by the City Surveyor, on the owners or occupants of premises in front of or adjacent to the avenue or street directed to be graded, paved, or planked. Funds to plank or grade or pave streets—how raised.

SEC. 17. The said City Surveyor shall make a separate assessment on the lots or premises so assessed, as aforesaid, for the grading, paving, or planking any cross street or avenue, in such proportions as he shall deem just and equitable, provided each block shall only be assessed to the centre of such cross street or avenue, each way. Assessment for cross streets.

SEC. 18. The manner of making said assessments, and all other subsequent proceedings in the premises, shall be the same as are required under the provisions of sections six, seven, and nine of this chapter, except that the notice be given by the City Clerk, under the provisions of section seven, shall notify persons to be assessed that they are about to be assessed to defray the expenses of grading, paving, or planking the street or streets and alleys adjacent to certain premises owned or occupied by them, &c. How assessment for paving and planking made.

SEC. 19. If the owners or occupants shall omit to grade, pave, or plank said avenues or streets in front of or adjacent to their respective lots or premises, or pay their proportion of the assessment for grading, paving, or planking any cross street, avenue, or alleys, so that the expenses of all grading done shall be assessed upon the property fronting the same, within such time as the Common Council may by resolution direct, then the said Common Council may issue their warrant for the collection of said assessment, and all costs and charges thereon, and on failure of the proper officer to collect the same, the said lots or premises shall be sold agreeably to the provisions of these ordinances, "Relative to the collection of special assessments." Collection of assessments

SEC. 20. Such avenues or streets, or such portions thereof as the Common Council may direct to be planked, shall be done with good sound pine, oak, or hemlock plank, not less than four inches in thickness, nor more than ten inches in width, said planks to be spiked or pinned down solid, on timbers not less than four inches in thickness, nor eight inches in width, of the same material, and firmly imbedded Of what materials plank roads to be constructed.

in the earth, so that the lower surface of the plank shall rest on the earth as well as the bed timbers, which shall be put down not more than four feet apart, said planks to be laid crosswise in the said avenues or streets, and the ends placed firmly against the curb-stones of the sidewalks, so as to leave the upper surface of the planks five inches below the top of the curb-stones, and the corner to be filled with one-half of a stick of timber five inches square, sawed through the extreme corners, the back well fitted to the curb, and spiked down solid to the plank, so as to prevent the water from washing the sand from between the curb-stones and pavement. All planks to be laid according to the established grade of the avenue or street. The work to be done to the satisfaction of the Common Council, or such committee as they shall appoint to inspect the same.

Crosswalks.

Assessments for repairing and constructing crosswalks.

SEC. 21. The expense of construction and the repairs of all crosswalks over the streets and alleys of the city, hereafter to be made, and not already provided for, shall be defrayed by a rateable assessment upon the real property of one quarter of each of the blocks so to be connected, and being that half respectively which lies in the line of direction of the crosswalk; and said assessment shall be taken from the general assessment roll of the city for the current year.

When Council to direct construction of crosswalks

SEC. 22. Whenever a majority of the taxable inhabitants of each of any two blocks to be connected, shall petition the Common Council to have a crosswalk constructed to connect said blocks, the Common Council will order the construction of such crosswalk at such point or points of connection as the petitioners may designate, and of the width prayed for; and whenever a less number than such majority shall so petition, or the Common Council shall direct without petition, the construction of such walk shall not be ordered, except upon a report thereon by the Committee on the Streets of said city.

Street Commissioner to construct crosswalks and warrant to issue for collection of assessment for the same.

SEC. 23. As soon as a crosswalk shall be ordered, in pursuance of the foregoing provisions, the Street Commissioner shall proceed without delay to construct the same, but at a rate not exceeding the usual relative rates paid by the city for similar constructions, and the City Surveyor shall report the assessment for constructing the same at the next succeeding meeting of the Common Council, for confirmation, and upon such confirmation, a warrant shall issue for the amount of said assessment, and the Street Commissioner shall proceed at once to collect the same.

Repairs.

SEC. 24. All sidewalks in the city of Detroit shall be kept in good repair by the owner or occupant of the house, lot, or premises adjoining or fronting on such, and whenever any sidewalk within the limits of said city shall require repairing, it shall be the duty of the Street Commissioner of the district in which the same is situated to notify by a written or printed, or a partly written or partly printed notice, the owner or occupant of such house, lot, or other premises adjacent to or fronting on such parts of said sidewalk, needing such repairs, to repair the same within forty-eight hours, and if the person thus notified shall refuse or neglect to comply with the exigency of said notice, then the said Street Commissioner shall have said repairs made, and shall report the making of the same to the City Surveyor, who shall prepare and transmit to the Common Council a proper assessment roll, assessing the expense of said repairs upon said lot or premises, which roll shall be confirmed by the Common Council in the same manner as other special assessments: *Provided, however,* That where the said Commissioner shall estimate that the expense of any repair herein provided for will exceed the sum of two hundred dollars, he shall report the fact of notice and the estimate of expense to the said Common Council, who shall then provide for the making of said repair by contract, as is prescribed by law. It shall be the duty of said Street Commissioners to keep in a book a copy of all notices served under this section, on which shall be made a memorandum, signed by the Commissioner serving the notice, of the time when, the person on whom, and the manner in which, said notice was served. If any lot or premises in front of or adjacent to which said repairs shall be required, shall be unoccupied, and the owner or owners, or lessee thereof cannot be found in the city of Detroit, said Street Commissioner may serve said notice to repair by posting the same in some conspicuous position upon said lot or premises.

When Street Commissioner to notify owners to repair, &c.

City Surveyor to make roll.

Proviso.

SEC. 25. All expenses for making assessments under this chapter or any other ordinance, together with the expense of printing notices, and all other charges relating to such assessments, shall be justly apportioned by the City Treasurer to the persons liable to pay said assessments, and shall be collected at the same time.

Expense of making assessment to be paid by the person assessed.

TITLE II. CHAPTER 12.

The Council may authorize any other person to do the duty of Street Commissioner.

SEC. 26. The Common Council may at any time, by resolution, to be entered on their journal, authorize or require any person or officer of the corporation of said city, to perform the same duties which are hereinbefore required to be performed by the Street Commissioner, or other officer.

Penalty for injuring Streets, &c.

SEC. 27. Any person or persons who shall in any manner be guilty of a wanton injury to any side or crosswalk, paving or planking, within the limits of the city, by impairing, destroying, or removing the same, or any part thereof, shall, on conviction thereof in the Recorder's Court, be subject to a fine not exceeding fifty dollars.

Forms of proceeding under this chapter.

SEC. 28. The following or other sufficient forms shall be used in proceedings under the provisions of this chapter:

No. 1.

RESOLUTION.

Resolved, That a plank sidewalk, (or brick or stone sidewalk, as the case may be,) be constructed on   street in this city, between   and   , and that the City Surveyor make an assessment of the expense of the same, according to the ordinance in such case made and provided.

No. 2.

Assessment Roll for Constructing a Plank Sidewalk from   to   in the City of Detroit, on the   year A. D. 18 .

Names of Residents.	Names of Non-Residents.	Description of lots.	Width of Walk.	Length of Walk.	Amount of Tax.	Costs of assess't.	Final costs.	Total.

To the Hon. the Common Council:

I herewith report to your Hon. body the foregoing report or assessment as correct and just.

Dated at Detroit, this   day   A. D. 18 .

City Surveyor.

[Let the assessment roll be filed by the Clerk.]

No. 3.

Notice to Persons to be Assessed.

STATE OF MICHIGAN, } ss.
City of Detroit. }

To (here insert the names of those to whom directed, and add,) *or to any other person interested in the premises, within the limits hereafter mentioned :*

You are hereby notified that assessments are about to be made upon you to defray the expenses of constructing plank sidewalks, (or paving the sidewalks, or streets, as the case may be,) in front of, or adjacent to certain premises or lots of land owned or occupied by you respectively, on street, in the city of Detroit, State of Michigan; and also, that a report or assessment roll has been made in the premises, which is on file in the office of the Clerk of said city, where it will remain open for your inspection until the day of A. D. 18 , when and where you may appear and show cause before the Common Council, in the Common Council house in said city, why the said assessment should not be made and collected according to law.

By order of the Common Council,

——————, *City Clerk.*

Dated at the city of Detroit, }
this day of A. D. 18 . }

[After the time mentioned in the notice, and on filing affidavit thereof, let a resolution of the following form be entered on the journal.]

Whereas, It appears by affidavit on file, that due notice has been given to the owners and occupants of premises fronting on street in the city of Detroit, that the Common Council would, on the day of A. D. 18 , meet and review the report or assessment roll filed by the City Clerk on the day of A. D. 18 , for the expense of constructing in front of said premises: *And whereas,* No person has appeared before the Common Council, to object to said assessment, or the confirmation thereof; (if there be any objection, say after the word "whereas"—all objections thereto have been duly considered,) therefore

Resolved, That said assessment roll is hereby approved and confirmed; that the description of premises and the names of persons contained therein, are received as correct; and that the sums which

TITLE II. CHAPTER 13.

the said assessment roll states to be the correct ones, which each individual, or set of individuals, should be assessed at and pay, be the assessment, and be collected from the several persons liable to pay the same according to law.

[Then let the Clerk endorse on the roll, the words: "Approved and confirmed by the Common Council, this day of A. D. 18 ."

CHAPTER XIII.

Relative to the manner of obtaining possession of Lots sold for Taxes.

Possession of lots under tax title, how obtained.

SECTION 1. Whenever the title of any person shall become absolute by virtue of the sale or lease of any lot or parcel of land in said city, in pursuance of the second section of an act, entitled "An act to amend the several acts relative to the city of Detroit," approved April 22, 1833, such person, his legal representative or attorney, shall make demand in writing of the person in possession, and notify him that he claims possession of such lot, by virtue of a sale or lease under said section.

Persons refusing to deliver possession may be cited before Recorder's Court.

SEC. 2. If the person in possession shall neglect or refuse for the space of six days after such demand, to give up possession of such lot, then the person claiming the same may present a petition to the Recorder's Court of said city, verified by his own oath, or by some person for him, setting forth his right to such possession, and praying that a citation may issue, directed to the person in possession; upon filing such petition, the Court may order that a citation issue accordingly, which shall be issued, and be returnable in the same manner as a summons: *Provided*, The petitioner enter into a bond to the Corporation of the city of Detroit, with such sureties as the Court shall direct, conditioned to pay all costs that may accrue in such proceedings.

Proceedings to obtain possession of lots leased by the city.

SEC. 3. If the defendant appears, he may plead the general issue, and give notice of any special matter which he intends to give in evidence.

Forcible Entry and Detainer.

Whenever, according to the laws of the State, relative to forcible entry and detainer, the corporation of said city are entitled to the possession of any lands and tenements, the same proceedings shall be had in such case in the Recorder's Court of said city, so far as the same apply, as are authorized before Justices of the Peace. *Provided*, That in all cases the Marshal of said city shall give notice in writing to the persons in possession to quit the same, and in default thereof for the space of six days thereafter, the Marshal shall make report thereof to the City Attorney.

TITLE THREE.

OF STREETS AND ALLEYS.

CHAPTER XIV.

Relative to the use of Streets and Alleys.

No vehicle to be kept in the streets.

SECTION 1. No person shall leave any wagon, cart, carriage, sleigh or any vehicle, standing or remaining in any of the public streets of said city, the same not being in use at the time, under a penalty not exceeding ten dollars and costs for every offence.

No horses to be kept in the streets; carts to have lock chains.

SEC. 2. No person shall leave any horse or horses in any of the public streets of said city, without being sufficiently tied; nor shall any person be permitted to use a cart within the limits of said city, unless such cart is provided with a chain to lock the wheel; any person offending against either of these provisions shall be subject to pay a fine not exceeding five dollars and costs, for every offence.

Certain obstructions unlawful.

SEC. 3. No person shall place, or cause to be placed, any stone, timber, lumber, planks, boards or other materials in or upon any of the public streets, lanes or alleys of said city, unless for the purpose of building; and then only for a period of time not exceeding four months, without leave had of the Mayor or Common Council; any person offending against either of these provisions, shall, for every offence, be subject to pay a penalty not exceeding fifty dollars and costs.

Penalty for

Obstructions occasioned by buildings.

SEC. 4. No person so building shall obstruct the gutters or more than one-half of the sidewalk, and one-quarter of the carriage way of

TITLE III. CHAPTER 14.

Penalty for

said street opposite the lot owned by such person, under a penalty not exceeding twenty-five dollars, and a further penalty not exceeding five dollars for every forty-eight hours that any such sidewalk, gutter or street shall afterwards remain obstructed.

Building materials to be removed when build'g is finished.

SEC. 5. After the completion of any building, but within the period of four months aforesaid, (unless otherwise permitted by the Mayor or Common Council,) all building materials and rubbish arising therefrom, shall be removed from the street; and any person offending in the premises, shall be liable to pay a penalty not exceeding five dollars for every forty-eight hours such materials or rubbish shall be or remain in such street, after the time limited aforesaid, and costs.

Penalty for not removing

How drains, water pipes, &c., laid; penalty.

SEC. 6. It shall not be lawful for any person to make or construct any drain or sewer, or lay down any water pipes in any of the public streets of said city, within at least four feet of the curb stone of the sidewalks, unless it shall be the side drain, sewer or water pipe leading to or from the building or lot for which it is designed; any person offending against this provision shall be liable to be fined a sum not exceeding twenty dollars and costs.

Damages occasioned by excavations to be repaired

SEC. 7. Whenever it shall be necessary for any person, with a view to construct or make any such drain or sewer, or lay down any water pipes, or for any other purpose whatsoever, to tear up any pavement, side or crosswalk, or to dig any hole, ditch or drain, in any of the public streets of said city, it shall be the duty of such person, as speedily as practicable, to repair and put all such pavements, side or crosswalks, and streets in as good order and condition as the same were in previously; to pound down the earth so as to make it firm and solid; and as often as the earth shall settle to repair the same; but it shall not be lawful for any person or persons (except the Board of Water Commissioners, by consent of the Committee on Streets and Sewers,) within the limits of said city to excavate, dig or take up any pavement or paved street, side or crosswalk, or to dig any hole, ditch or drain upon any of the public pavements or paved streets, or for any other purpose whatsoever in said city, without having obtained the written consent of the Street Commissioner, upon written application to said Street Commissioner, signed by the person or persons making application for the same; any person offending against any of the provisions of this section shall be subject to pay a penalty for every offence, not exceeding twenty dollars and costs.

Owner or occupants to clear gutters.

SEC. 8. It shall be the duty of every owner or occupant of any house or other building or premises, in the city of Detroit, at all times to keep the drain or gutter in front of the same clear and free from any obstruction that may hinder the free passage of water; any person offending in the premises, shall be liable to pay a fine not exceeding ten dollars for every offence, and costs.

Rubbish, &c., not to be thrown into gutters, and no drains shall lead into streets and alleys.

SEC. 9. No person shall cast or throw, or cause to be thrown into any of the drains, sewers or gutters within said city, any straw, shavings, wood, stones, rubbish, or any filth or other substance, or cause any obstruction, nuisance or injury in or to the same, by diverting or stopping the water course thereof, or otherwise, under a penalty not exceeding ten dollars and costs for every offence; nor shall any person drain, or permit to be drained, from any lot or cellar owned or occupied by him or her, within the limits of this city, into, or on the surface of any streets or alleys of said city, the water from his or her lot or cellar, under a penalty not exceeding one hundred dollars and costs of prosecution.

Nuisances not to be placed in streets.

SEC. 10. No person shall throw, place or deposit, or suffer his or her servant, child or family, to throw, place or deposit any dung, dead animal, carrion, putrid meat or fish, entrails or decayed vegetables, or nuisance of any kind, nor shall he knowingly suffer the same to remain in any street or lane of said city; and any person who shall violate any of the prohibitions of this section, shall forfeit and pay a fine not to exceed five dollars for each offence, and costs of prosecution. The finding of any of the articles named in this section, in front or rear, or side of any lot, shall be *prima facie* evidence that the same were placed there by the occupant or occupants of said lot; and the burden of proof shall rest on the defendant.

Excavations when made—how protected.

SEC. 11. No person shall hereafter be permitted to make any excavation in any of the streets or alleys of this city, for any purpose whatever, between the fifteenth day of October and the fifteenth day of April thereafter, unless by special leave of the Common Council; and no excavation in any of the streets or alleys of the city shall be made at any time, unless the person or persons making the same, or causing the same to be made, shall erect a suitable guard or fence about such excavation, and shall, during the night time, cause lights to be attached and maintained to and upon such guard or fence, proper and sufficient to warn all persons passing by or near the same, or ap-

Penalty.

proaching the same, of the existence of such obstruction or excavation. Any person or persons violating the provisions of this section, shall forfeit a sum of not exceeding one hundred dollars and costs of prosecution, to be recovered in the Recorder's Court, and shall also be liable for damages to any person or persons injured in the premises, in their person or property.

Streets and alleys not to be used for labor.

SEC. 12. It shall not be lawful for any carpenter, stone mason or other person, to use or occupy any street, lane or alley in the said city, for the purpose of framing timber, or for cutting, sawing or dropping stone, unless by permission of the Common Council of said city, and all persons offending against the provisions of this section, on conviction thereof before the Recorder's Court, shall pay a fine not exceeding twenty-five dollars for every such offence.

Penalty.

No obstructions to be left in the streets at night.

SEC. 13. It shall not be lawful for any person to leave any cart or carriage or sleigh, wood, timber, or any other incumbrance or obstruction, in any of the lanes or alleys of the said city, during the night season, and any person offending herein, on conviction before the Recorder's Court, shall pay a fine not exceeding twenty dollars, and it shall be the duty of the Marshal to remove all such obstructions.

Rate of driving.

SEC. 14. No person or persons shall run or race any horse or horses, or drive any carriage or vehicle of any kind within the limits of the city of Detroit, at a faster rate than six miles per hour, under a penalty for each offence not exceeding ten dollars and costs.

Cattle.

SEC. 15. It shall not be lawful for any person to drive, herd together, or detain in any of the streets, lanes or alleys of this city, any cattle, horses, sheep, hogs or goats, for any purpose whatever, under a penalty for each offence, not exceeding twenty dollars and costs: *Provided*, That this section shall not extend to sales at auction, under the laws of this State.

Stud horses, penalty for displaying.

SEC. 16. No person shall display and detain for public exhibition, in any of the said streets, lanes or alleys, any stud horse, under a penalty for each offence not exceeding twenty dollars and costs.

Flying kites prohibited.

SEC. 17. No person or persons shall raise or fly any kite in any of the streets or alleys aforesaid, or within the limits of the said city, under a penalty for every offence not exceeding twenty dollars and costs of prosecution.

Earth not to be removed from streets.

SEC. 18. No person or persons shall, unless authorized specially by the Common Council, dig, remove, or carry away any earth, loam, sand, gravel or sod, from any of the public grounds within the limits of the city of Detroit, under a penalty for each offence not exceeding fifty dollars, with costs of prosecution.

Parents and employees liable for certain offences.

SEC. 19. In all cases where any hired servant, apprentice or minor shall be guilty of any breach of the foregoing sections, the master, mistress, employer, parent or guardian of such person so guilty, shall be responsible for the aforesaid penalty.

Marshal and constables to arrest under this chapter.

SEC. 20. That the Marshal and all the Constables of this city are required and directed to notice all infringements of this chapter, and forthwith to arrest and bring before any member of the Common Council all persons guilty of any breach thereof, who shall thereupon give sufficient bail for their appearance at the ensuing term of the Recorder's Court, or on default thereof, to be committed to custody until the holding of said court.

Not lawful to occupy the streets with shantees, &c.

SEC. 21. It shall not be lawful for any person or persons to occupy any portion or part of the public streets or sidewalks with any tent, shanty, shop, table or building, wagon or cart, wheelbarrows and horses, for the retail sale of any liquors, groceries, cakes, pies or merchandise. And any person offending against the provisions of this section, shall, on conviction, be fined in a sum not exceeding five dollars and costs of prosecution; and it shall be the duty of the Marshal to remove such tent, shanty, shop, table or building, cart or wagon, as a public nuisance: *Provided*, Nothing in this section contained, shall be construed to interfere with the ordinances relative to markets or bakers supplying their regular customers.

Vehicles not to block side walks.

SEC. 22. It shall not be lawful for any person to have or keep for an unreasonable time, any cart, wagon, dray or other vehicle, on any of the crosswalks in any street or alley of said city, under a penalty for each offence not exceeding fifty dollars and costs of prosecution.

No nuisance permitted in the streets.

SEC. 23. No person shall knowingly permit or suffer his property to be and remain in any street or alley of said city, so as to become a nuisance, under a penalty for each offence not exceeding fifty dollars and costs of prosecution, together with the expense of removing such nuisance.

NOTE.—This Ordinance has been nearly superseded by the following.

TITLE III. CHAPTER 15.

CHAPTER XV.

Relative to the use of Streets and Alleys.

S't Comm'rs to order the removal of all obstructions on streets, sidewalks, &c.

SECTION 1. That the Street Commissioners of the city of Detroit, or either of them, are hereby authorized to order any article or thing whatever, which may encumber or obstruct any street or sidewalk in said city, to be removed; and in case the same shall not be removed within twenty-four hours after notice to remove the same, to cause the same to be carried or removed to such place as the Common Council of said city may designate and provide for the purpose; and it shall be the duty of the said Street Commissioners, in case the said order is not obeyed, to complain of the person or persons who have placed or maintained said article or thing in said street, or upon said sidewalk.

To remove the same and enter complaint.

To order the removal of step-stones, fences, &c., within a reasonable time.

SEC. 2. The said Street Commissioners, or either of them, are hereby authorized, whenever they shall deem it proper, to order any step-stone used for entering carriages, any railing or fence, any sign, sign-post or other post, any area, bay window, or other window, any porch, cellar, door, platform, stoop or step, or any other thing which may encumber or obstruct any street, to be altered or removed therefrom, within such time as shall be reasonable and limited by said Street Commissioners, or either of them, when ordered by the Common Council.

Notice to be in writing.

SEC. 3. The order of direction, mentioned in the last preceding section, shall be in writing, and shall be served personally, or by leavit at the house or place of business of the owner, occupant or person having charge of the house or lot in front of which such step-stone or other encumbrance may be.

To enter complaint.

SEC. 4. If any person, notified in accordance with the last preceding section, shall neglect or refuse to obey or comply with said notice, the Street Commissioner serving such notice shall complain of such person, and if upon said complaint said person shall be convicted, then said person shall be punished by a fine of not more than ten dollars, or by not more than ten days' imprisonment, and in addition thereto, shall be fined five dollars for each and every day from and after the time limited and appointed in said notice, until the same shall have been complied with.

Penalty for disobeying notice.

SEC. 5. All articles or things carted or removed, as is provided in the first section of this ordinance, shall be advertised by ten days' notice in the official paper of the City, and sold by the Street Commissioner who so carted or removed them, and he shall retain so much of the proceeds of said sale to pay the expenses of said cartage or removal, and sale, together with the cost of advertising, and six cents per day for every day that each cart load of said article or thing shall have remained in the place designated and provided by the Common Council, to which the same shall have been removed, and the balance, if any, of the proceeds of said sale, shall be paid to the City Treasurer of said city, and shall be paid by him to such person or persons as shall exhibit satisfactory proof of the ownership of such articles or things sold as aforesaid; and each of said Street Commissioners shall keep a regular account of all such articles and things sold by him as aforesaid, and shall once in each quarter account with the Controller, under oath, for his receipts and disbursements under this section.

Ten days' notice of sale to be given.

Balance of proceeds of sale, after deducting expenses, to be paid City Treasurer, and by him to the owner of property sold.

Comm'rs to keep an account.

SEC. 6. All persons who may wish hereafter to erect balustrades or balconies, extending beyond the line of and overhanging any street, shall first obtain a permit so to do from the Common Council. Iron braces and railings shall be used for the construction of said balustrades and balconies, and it shall be the duty of the Street Commissioner of the District to test the strength of said balustrades and balconies when built, and if he shall deem them unsafe and dangerous, he shall order the same te be removed, and the person erecting the same shall obey said order; any person who shall violate the provisions of this section shall be punished by a fine not to exceed one hundred dollars, or by ninety days' imprisonment.

Persons erecting balconies, &c., to obtain a permit.

Materials to be used in constructi'n.

Penalty.

SEC. 7. No person shall leave any wagon, cart, carriage, sleigh or any vehicle, standing or remaining in the public streets of said city, the same not being in use at the time; no person shall leave any horse or horses not sufficiently tied and fastened in any of the public streets of said city; no person shall race any horse or horses in the public streets of said city; no person shall drive any carriage, cart or vehicle of any kind in said streets at a faster rate than six miles an hour; no person shall drive any horse or horses around a corner of any public street faster than a walk; no person shall display and detain for exhibition any stud horse, in the public streets of said city; no person shall place or stop his horse or horses, carts, carriage or other ve-

Wagons, horses, &c., not to be left standing in streets.

Racing and fast driving forbidden.

Stud horses not to be exhibited in streets.

TITLE III. CHAPTER 15.

Vehicles not to stop on crosswalks. hicle upon any crosswalk in any public street of said city; no person shall drive, or back, or lead any horse, or cart, or other wheel carriage, on the footpaths or sidewalks of any public street of said city; no owner or occupant of any store or house, shall permit or suffer any cart or other wheel carriage, to be driven or otherwise to pass or go over and upon the footpath or sidewalk opposite and in front of said store or house, for the purpose of loading or unloading said cart or other wheel carriage; and any person violating any of the provisions of this section shall be punished by a fine not to exceed fifty dollars, or by ninety days' imprisonment.

Carts, &c., not to be driven on sidewalks.

Penalty.

Kites, marbles, ten pins, &c. SEC. 8. No person shall raise or fly any kite in any public street of said city, or engage in any game of marbles, or nine or ten pins, or ball or wicket, in said streets; no persons shall gather in crowds, and stand upon or occupy the sidewalks of any public streets, so as to obstruct or encumber the same; and any person violating the provisions of this section shall be punished by a fine not to exceed fifty dollars, or by not more than thirty days' imprisonment.

Crowds in streets.

Penalty.

Obstruction of gutters, drains, &c. SEC. 9. No person shall cast or throw, or cause to be cast or thrown, into any of the drains, gutters or sewers within said city, straw, shavings, wood, stones, rubbish, or any filth, or other substance, or cause any obstruction, nuisance or injury in and to the same, by diverting or stopping the water thereof, or otherwise; no person shall drain or cause or permit to be drained, any water, filth or mud, from any lot or cellar owned or occupied by him or her, into or on the surface of any street or alley of said city; no person shall throw, place or deposit, or suffer his or her servant, child or family, to throw, place or deposit any dung, dead animal, carrion, putrid meat or fish, entrails, or decayed vegetables, slops, swill, dish water, or stinking, unwholesome or disgusting substance of any kind into any public street or alley of said city; nor shall said person knowingly suffer the same to remain in said street or alley, and the finding of the same in the front, rear or side of any lot, shall be *prima facie* evidence that the same was placed there by the occupant or occupants of the lot; no person shall make water, or deposit his or her excrement, in any public street of said city; or erect, maintain or use any privy or backhouse, on the line of and adjacent to a public street; and any person violating the provisions of this section, shall be punished by a fine not

No person to drain into public streets and alleys.

No filthy substance to be thrown in streets or alleys.

No person to make water in the public streets.

Privies not to be built on streets.

Penalty.

to exceed one hundred dollars, or by not more than ninety days' imprisonment.

Excavations—when forbidden, when allowed, and by whom.

SEC. 10. No person shall make any excavation in any of the public streets of said city, for any purpose, between the fifteenth day of November and the fifteenth day of April, in each year, unless by special leave granted by the Common Council; and no person shall make any excavation in said streets at any other time in said year, without the written permission of the Committee on Streets, or said Common Council, and of the Street Commissioner of the District in which said excavation is to be made; and no excavation shall be made at any time unless the person or persons making the same, or causing the same to be made, shall erect a suitable guard or fence about such excavation, and shall, during the night time, cause lights to be attached and maintained to and upon such guard or fence, proper and sufficient to warn all persons passing by or near the same, or approaching the same, of the existence of such obstruction and excavation; and it shall be the duty of the Street Commissioner of the District to see that guards and lights are properly constructed and maintained. Any person violating the provisions of this section shall be punished by a fine not to exceed one hundred dollars, or by not more than ninety days' imprisonment.

Suitable guards to be erected and lights thereon at night.

S't Comm'r, duties of.

Penalty for neglect.

S't Comm'r, duties of in regard to pavement.

SEC. 11. No person shall tear up or remove any pavement or sidewalk in any public street in said city, without the written permission of the Street Commissioner of the District in which said pavement or sidewalk is situated; no person shall in any way injure or destroy said pavement, or pave any street in said city, unless with the consent and under the direction of the City Pavior or Common Council of said city; the City Pavior shall receive for his services, from said person, such compensation as may be fixed by the Common Council of said city; and any person violating the provisions of this section shall be punished by a fine not to exceed one hundred dollars, or by not more than ninety days' imprisonment.

City Pavior to do the work.

Compensat'n

Penalty.

Distance fr'm curb at which pipes, &c., are to be laid down.

SEC. 12. No person shall make or construct any drain or sewer, or lay down any water pipes in any of the public streets of said city, within at least four feet of the curb stone of the sidewalks, unless it shall be side drain, sewer, or water pipe leading to or from the lot or building for which it is designed, and connecting with some public sewer, water main or gas pipes, permitted to be laid and maintained in said

Exceptions.

TITLE III. CHAPTER 15.

Penalty.

streets; and any person violating the provisions of this section shall be punished by a fine not to exceed one hundred dollars, or by not more than ninety days' imprisonment.

All excavations to be repaired at the expense of the persons making the same.

SEC. 13. Whenever it shall be necessary for any person, with a view to construct or make any such drain or sewer, or lay down any water pipes, or for any purposes whatsoever, to tear up any pavement, side or crosswalk, or to dig any hole, ditch or drain in any of the public streets of said city, it shall be the duty of such person at his own expense, as speedily as practicable, to put all such pavements, sidewalks or streets in as good order as they were previously, and to pound down the earth from the bottom of any excavation he has made, solid, so that it shall present a firm surface, and as often as said earth shall settle, to pound and fill the same, until it shall finally be accepted and approved by the City Pavior, who shall be paid for his services by said person; and any person violating the provisions of this section shall be punished by a fine of not more than ten dollars, or by not more than five days' imprisonment, besides being liable in any action at law to the City for any actual damage done.

Penalty.

Council may grant permit to place building materials in street.

SEC. 14. No person shall place, or cause to be placed, any materials for building in or upon any public street or alley of said city, without the permission of the Common Council; no person so building shall obstruct the gutters, or more than one half of the sidewalk and one-quarter of the carriage way of said street opposite the lot owned by such person; no person thus occupying any street shall occupy any portion thereof save a strip of the width, and opposite to the frontage on said street, of the lot on which he is erecting any building; and after the completion of said building, the person erecting the same shall forthwith remove from the street all building material, dirt and rubbish, arising therefrom, and shall put said street in complete order, cleanliness and repair; and any person violating the provisions of this section shall be punished by a fine not to exceed one hundred dollars, or by not more than ninety days' imprisonment.

Quantity to be occupied by same.

Removal of rubbish, &c.

Penalty.

Other ordinances repealed.

SEC. 15. All ordinances or parts of ordinances contravening the provisions of this ordinance are hereby repealed.

CHAPTER XVI.

Relative to Cleaning Streets.

SECTION 1. The Committee on Streets and the City Controller are hereby authorized to contract with the lowest bidder, who shall propose to clean such portions of the paved or planked streets, squares or alleys, as the corporation are liable to clean.

Committee on Streets and City Controller authorized to contract with suitable persons to clean streets.

SEC. 2. The said lowest bidder, or person contracting with the corporation as aforesaid, shall furnish satisfactory security for the performance of such contract, provided notice shall be published for one week, in the city paper, previous to receiving proposals for said work.

Such persons to furnish security.

CHAPTER XVII.

Relative to Sidewalks.

SECTION 1. That the following be established as the width of all sidewalks within the limits of the city of Detroit: Upon streets of one hundred and twenty feet and upwards in width, the sidewalks on each side of the street shall be of the width of twenty feet throughout, excepting Washington avenue, which shall be fifty feet; and also excepting that portion of Jefferson Avenue which lies between Beaubien street and the eastern line of the said city, which shall have on each side of said portion of said avenue, a sidewalk twenty-five feet wide; on streets of one hundred feet, the sidewalks shall be seventeen feet; on streets of eighty or ninety feet wide, the sidewalks shall be fifteen feet wide; on streets of seventy or seventy-two feet, the sidewalks shall be fifteen feet; on streets of sixty feet, the sidewalks shall be ten feet; on streets of fifty feet, the sidewalks shall be nine feet; and on streets of forty feet, the sidewalks shall be eight feet.

Dimensions of sidewalks.

SEC. 2. No person or persons shall place or cause to be placed upon any of the sidewalks of this city, any box, barrel, article of merchandize, or other obstructions whatsoever, except so far as the same be necessary and unavoidable in transporting such articles across the sidewalk; nor shall any person be allowed to place or cause to be placed on any stone pavement or flagging within the limits of said city, (except for the purpose of transporting the same across said

No obstructions to be placed upon sidewalks.

TITLE III. CHAPTER 17.

walk,) any barrels, kegs or boxes of salt, or of any other substance or material, by which said pavement or flagging may in any wise be injured, defaced or destroyed, under a penalty of twenty dollars for each offence.

Penalty for so doing.

Marshal to require persons to remove obstructions.

SEC. 3. It shall be the duty of the Marshal, upon knowledge or information that any of the sidewalks of the city are in any manner obstructed or encumbered, to require the occupant or occupants, owner or owners, of the lot or premises in front of which such encumbrance exists, to remove it; every such occupant or owner neglecting for the space of twenty-four hours to comply with such requisition, and every person wilfully offending against this section shall, on conviction thereof, be punished by fine not exceeding twenty-five dollars and costs.

When Marshal shall remove obstructions.

SEC. 4. It shall be the duty of the Marshal to remove all obstructions from the sidewalks in front of unoccupied lots or premises.

Awning posts permitted.

SEC. 5. The restrictions above written shall not extend to posts for awnings, shade trees, or the boxes to protect them, which are now standing, nor ladders which are necessarily used in the building or repair of houses, nor be construed to affect the ingress and egress to and from the yards of houses across said walks, unless otherwise ordered by the Common Council.

Horses to be kept off walks.

SEC. 6. Except for the purposes of ingress and egress, no person whatever shall drive, ride or lead any horse, cart or carriage of any kind on any of the sidewalks within this city, under a penalty not exceeding ten dollars for each offence, and being liable to repair and make good all damages caused by him or them; and if the party offending herein shall neglect to get the same repaired within twenty-four hours after the damage, it shall be the duty of the Overseer of Highways for the District to get said repairs made, and the expenses attendant thereon, with a sufficient recompense to the Overseer, shall be recovered of the party offending, in the same manner as the said penalty.

Sidewalks and gutter to be cleaned.

SEC. 7. From the first day of April to the first day of November in each year, every owner or occupant of any house or lot in any of the streets in which the sidewalks are now made or which shall hereafter be made (excepting such lots whereon buildings may be erecting, and on which materials for building are laid,) shall cause the sidewalk as well as the gutter to be swept, or otherwise cleaned, on every Saturday during the period aforesaid, under a penalty of one dollar for every omission. TITLE III. CHAPTER 17.

Mayor to appoint persons to clean streets.

SEC. 8. The Mayor shall from time to time appoint so many persons as he may think proper, who shall exclusively have the right and enjoy the emoluments of cleaning on each Monday, or as soon thereafter as is practicable, such parts of the sidewalks and gutters as shall not have been cleaned on the previous Saturday; and the Mayor shall designate to each person so appointed, what part of the city it shall be his duty to attend, for the purpose aforesaid.

To be clean'd at the expense of occupant or owner.

SEC. 9. In case the owner or occupant of any house or lot shall neglect to sweep or otherwise clean such sidewalks and gutters on the day directed by this chapter to be done by him or her, it shall be lawful for the person or persons whom the Mayor shall appoint for that purpose, on every succeeding Monday to sweep or otherwise clean such sidewalk and gutter, and for which he shall be entitled to demand twenty-five cents from the owner or occupant of such house or lot, who, on paying said sum, shall be exonerated from the payment of the penalty incurred as aforesaid; but if the said owner or occupant of any such house or lot shall neglect or refuse to pay the said twenty-five cents to such person appointed, it shall be the duty of the Marshal immediately thereafter to cause such owner or occupant to be prosecuted for the penalty aforesaid.

Snow to be removed from walks.

SEC. 10. The owner or occupant aforesaid shall cause the sidewalks fronting their respective premises, between the first day of November and the first day of April, to be kept free and clear from snow and ice, by sweeping or otherwise removing the same, within twenty-four hours after the said snow shall have fallen, or the ice formed, and in case of any omission, the same penalty shall attach, and the same remedy be applied, as is provided in the preceding sections for sweeping and cleaning the sidewalks and gutters.

TITLE III. CHAPTER 18.

CHAPTER XVIII.

Relative to Awning and Sign Posts.

Posts for telegraphs, &c., to be put up under the direction of S't Comm'r.

SECTION 1. No post, except for the purpose of supporting awning or telegraph wires, or hitching horses, shall be erected or put up in any paved street, road, lane or alley of the city of Detroit, unless under the direction of the Street Commissioner, under a penalty of five dollars, in the discretion of the Court, and costs of prosecution, for each offence.

Penalty.

No wooden posts allowed in certain places.

SEC. 2. No wooden post, for the purpose of supporting any awning, shall be erected, or placed upon or before any paved street, lane, road or alley in this city, under a penalty of ten dollars, in the discretion of the Court, and costs of prosecution, for each day such post shall be suffered to remain, after notice to the owner or occupant of the premises from the Mayor, Committee on Streets, Street Commissioner or Marshal, to remove the same.

Penalty.

Awning posts on paved streets of what made and how.

SEC. 3. All posts erected or fixed in any paved street, lane, road or alley, for the purpose of supporting any awning, shall be of iron, and of a uniform style, to be made after a certain pattern to be kept in the office of the Street Commissioner, and approved by the Common Council; and such posts shall be placed next to and alongside of the curb stone, and be not less than eight feet in height, or of such height as may be determined on by a resolution of the Common Council. Nor shall any person or persons, place or cause to be placed, or suffer to remain across any of the sidewalks within the limits of the city, (except as hereinafter provided in section 4,) rails, or strips of boards, or bars, connecting any posts placed alongside the curb stones, with buildings, or any posts, or erection, by the side of any building or buildings, from which any awning or awnings may be suspended, on which to roll up such awnings, or for any other purpose, unless the same be removed when the awning is taken down. Any person violating the provisions of this section, shall pay a fine of not more than ten nor less than three dollars, in the discretion of the Court, and costs of prosecution, for each day he shall so offend.

Penalty.

Rails connecting awning posts with building prohibited.

SEC. 4. No person shall place, or cause to be placed, any rails or bars connecting said iron posts with buildings, except so far as may be necessary to brace said posts, under the supervision of the Street Commissioner, and said rails or bars shall be removed when the awnings are taken down, under penalty of five dollars for each offence, and costs of prosecution. Penalty.

SEC. 5. No portion of any awning, cloth or canvass used as an awning, shall hang loosely down from the same, within eight feet of the sidewalk or crossing, under a penalty of ten dollars, in the discretion of the Court, and costs of prosecution, for each day that the provisions of this section shall be violated. Awning cloths not to hang. Penalty.

SEC. 6. No person shall place or cause to be placed, or shall suspend or cause to be suspended, from any house, shop, store, lot or place, over any street, any sign, lamp, goods, clothes, wares and merchandise, or wares or any other obstructions whatsoever, except frames for the support of awnings, so that the same shall extend or project from the wall or front of such house, shop, store, lot or place, more than three feet towards or into the street. No canvass, for the purpose of an awning, shall hereafter be erected or suspended from any store, house, building or lot, along side of, or adjacent to any paved street, lane or alley, unless the same shall be of sufficient length to project from the front of the building to the outer curb stone of said walk, under a penalty of ten dollars, in the discretion of the Court, and costs of prosecution, for each violation of the provisions of this section. Certain obstructions prohibited. Penalty.

SEC. 7. No person shall lay or place, or cause to be laid or placed, any coal, wood, merchandise, box, barrel, or other obstruction, upon any sidewalk or crossing, unless for the purpose of removing the same into or out from some store, shop, house, lot or place, and then the same shall not remain upon such sidewalk or crossing for a longer time than six hours, under a penalty of ten dollars, in the discretion of the Court, and costs of prosecution, for each violation of the provisions of this section. Certain articles not to be placed upon the walks.

CHAPTER XIX.

Relative to Digging Cellars.

SECTION 1. It shall not be lawful for any person to make and keep open in the front of any building on the line of the streets, any excavations for cellars, doors, windows, or areas to any cellar or basement story, of a greater width, including the front wall and ashlar, than How cellars may be dug.

TITLE III. CHAPTER 19.

seven feet, in streets of the breadth of one hundred feet and upwards, or of a greater width than one-third of the breadth of the sidewalks, as established by the existing ordinances of the said city in all other streets.

Areas to be closed while cellars are being dug.

SEC. 2. It shall be the duty of the owner of any building in the front of which any excavation or opening shall be made, or if such owner be a non-resident, of his agent or attorney, and also of the person or persons contracting or undertaking to execute the same, to cause such excavation to be well secured by a railing or covering, to the satisfaction of the Mayor, Recorder, or any of the Aldermen of the said city, during the prosecution of the work, and within thirty days after the completion of the same, to cause such excavation or opening to be secured by a substantial and permanent railing or enclosure, and all persons offending against the provisions of this chapter hereinbefore contained, on conviction thereof before the Recorder's Court, shall pay a fine not exceeding fifty dollars for every such offence.

When finished to be closed permanently.

Penalty.

Cellars in lanes, direction for digging.

SEC. 3. It shall not be lawful for any person to dig or cause to be dug, or to keep open, any cellarway or other opening in any lane or alley exceeding the width of three feet from the outer line or side of such lane or alley, and it shall be the duty of the person digging or causing to be dug such cellarway or opening, within five days after commencing the same, to cause it to be completed and secured with a substantial hatch or covering, laid even with the surface of said lane or alley, and all cellarways or openings already made in any lane or alley, shall be secured in like manner; and all persons offending against this section of this chapter, on conviction thereof before the Recorder's Court, shall pay a fine not exceeding twenty-five dollars for every such offence.

Excavations not in accordance with this chapter nuisances.

SEC. 4. All excavations or openings in any of the streets, lanes or alleys for the purpose aforesaid, which shall not be secured by a railing, hatch or covering as hereinbefore directed, or which shall hereafter be made or dug, contrary to the provisions and the true intent and meaning of this chapter, shall be taken and considered to be a common nuisance, and may be abated by order of the Mayor or Common Council of the said city at the expense of the said person or persons causing or suffering the same to remain.

SEC. 5. It shall be the duty of any person or persons taking up any pavement or sidewalk, or causing the same to be done in any street, lane or alley, for the aforesaid purposes, to replace and repair so much of the said pavement or sidewalk as is not included in said excavation or opening for cellar doors, windows or areas as aforesaid, in as good order and condition in all respects as they were in previously; and in case of the neglect or refusal of the person or persons whose duty it shall be to replace and repair the same, so to do, the said pavements or sidewalks may be replaced by order of the Mayor or Common Council of the said city, at the expense of the person or persons refusing or neglecting as aforesaid.

Pers ns taking up pavements to relay the same.

CHAPTER XX.

Relative to Numbering Buildings.

SECTION 1. Whenever the Common Council shall, by resolution, direct the public streets or avenues, or any part of said streets or avenues, to be numbered, said streets or avenues shall be numbered as hereinafter provided, and the owners or agents of the said buildings or premises so directed to be numbered, lying alongside said streets or avenues, shall pay the costs of numbering the same; and any owner or agent refusing or neglecting to have his premises or buildings so numbered, whenever a public street or avenue is directed to be numbered as aforesaid, such person or persons shall, for every such offence, on conviction before the Recorder's Court, forfeit a sum of five dollars and costs of prosecution.

Streets to be numbered when Council shall direct.

Penalty.

SEC. 2. That the numbering on Jefferson avenue, Woodbridge street, and Atwater street, commence at the western termination of each of said streets, and that the numbers one, three, five, seven, &c., be used on the left hand of each of said streets, and the numbers two, four, six, eight, &c., be used on the right hand of each of said streets, and proceed easterly as far as it may from time to time be deemed necessary or expedient.

How numbered.

SEC. 3. That on all streets parallel to Jefferson avenue, the numbering shall commence where such street crosses Woodward avenue, and proceed easterly and westerly, as far as necessary, using the odd numbers one, three, five, seven, &c., on the left, and even numbers,

Idem.

TITLE III. CHAPTER 21. two, four, six, eight, &c., on the right hand side of each of said streets.

Idem. SEC. 4. That on Woodward avenue, and all streets running parallel to it, the numbering shall commence at the channel of the Detroit river and proceed northerly as far as may be required, using the numbers one, three, five, seven, &c., on the left, and the numbers two, four, six, eight, &c., on the right hand side of each of said streets respectively.

Vacant lots how numbered. SEC. 5. That whenever there are vacant lots along the line of said streets, one number shall be allowed to every twenty feet of such vacant lot.

CHAPTER XXI.

Relative to Wharves.

To be kept in repair. SECTION 1. It shall be the duty of the owner or owners, occupant or occupants, lessee or lessees, of any of the wharves of this city, bordering upon the Detroit river, and which are not fenced in, or otherwise enclosed, so as to prevent the passage of travelers or others over or across them, to keep the same in good order and condition; and whenever any of the plank, boards, timber or other materials composing or forming a part of any of the wharves of said city, shall from any cause become loose, or be removed, or whenever any of said wharves shall in any manner, and from any cause whatever, be out of repair, it shall be the duty of the City Marshal to notify either the owner or owners, occupant or occupants, lessee or lessees, of any such wharf or wharves, to immediately replace and securely fasten the plank, board, or other material so removed as aforesaid, or otherwise to repair such wharf or wharves as to the Marshal may seem necessary: *Provided*, That the notice so to be given may be either a verbal or written notice, and may be given by either of the Constables, or by the Mayor, or any of the Aldermen, or other officers of the city; and if a written notice, it may be either served personally upon, or left at the place of business or residence of, the person or persons notified.

Marshal to notify to repair.

Penalty for not repairing. SEC. 2. In case the person or persons so notified, as provided for in the preceding section, shall neglect for twenty-four hours after such notice, to comply with the requisitions thereof, he, she or they shall, on conviction thereof before the Recorder's Court, be liable to a fine of not less than five, nor more than fifty dollars, for each and every day he, she or they shall neglect to comply with the requisitions of said notice.

CHAPTER XXII.

Relative to the Stationing, Anchoring, and Mooring of Vessels in the Detroit River.

Marshals and assistants Dock Masters.

SECTION 1. That the Marshal of said city shall be, and hereby is, made Dock Master of said city, for the purpose of directing the stationing, anchoring and mooring of vessels, agreeably to the provisions of this ordinance, within said city; and all policemen, assistant marshals, constables, or other officers appointed and paid by the city to serve, and stationed on any of the docks of said city, shall, at their respective stations, enforce the provisions of this ordinance.

Steamboats and vessels how long to remain at public wharf.

SEC. 2. No steamboat or vessel of any kind shall stop at or use any public wharf in said city for a longer space of time than one hour, nor shall any person land from said steamboat or vessel, or place upon any public wharf aforesaid, any article or thing, unless for the purpose of being immediately transported from said wharf to some other place; and if any article or thing so landed or placed upon said wharf shall remain there for the space of fifteen minutes after the same was so landed or placed on said wharf, the person so landing or placing the same on said wharf, and the owner, agent, captain, master, or any officer or employee of said steamboat or vessel, who actually landed, caused or directed to be landed, on said wharf, said article or thing, shall be punished by a fine not to exceed one hundred dollars, or by imprisonment not to exceed ninety days.

Goods landed to be immediately removed.

Certain articles not to be landed thereon.

SEC. 3. No person shall land or place upon any public wharf in said city any fire-wood, stones, brick, building materials, lime-bed, locomotives, cumbrous or heavy castings, or any material or thing calculated to injure or obstruct said wharf; and any person violating the provisions of this section shall be punished by a fine not to exceed one hundred dollars, or by imprisonment not to exceed ninety days.

SEC. 4. No steamboat or other vessel shall load or unload cargo,

Vessels, &c., not to repair at public wharves.

or lay out or receive ballast, or careen or be careened for repairs at any public wharf; and any person violating the provisions of this section shall be punished by a fine not to exceed one hundred dollars, or by imprisonment not to exceed ninety days.

City officers to remove goods so landed, and be placed in charge of S't Comm'r,

SEC. 5. The officers mentioned in the first section of this ordinance are authorized, whenever any article or thing is landed on any public wharf of said city, contrary to the provisions of this ordinance, to remove such article or thing to a place to be designated by the Common Council, which said article or thing shall remain in said place, in charge of the Street Commissioner of the district in which said article or thing was found, who shall receipt for the same to the officer bringing the same to him, and said article or thing shall be sold, and the proceeds of said sale disposed of and accounted for in the same manner, and the same costs and charges collected thereon, as is provided in regard to the sale of certain articles by section five of an ordinance relative to the use of streets and alleys.

Where ste'mboats and vessels to anchor.

SEC. 6. No steamboat or any other vessel shall anchor within one hundred feet of any wharf in said city; and if any person having charge of a steamboat or vessel shall anchor the same nearer to any wharf than one hundred feet, the said person shall be punished by a fine not to exceed one hundred dollars, or by imprisonment not to exceed ninety days: *Provided, always*, That nothing herein contained shall be construed to prevent any vessel from laying alongside of any dock with the consent of the owner of said dock.

Proviso.

Marshal and officers may board vessels to enforce this ordinance.

SEC. 7. The officers mentioned in the first section of this ordinance are hereby authorized to board any vessel or steamboat in the waters of the Detroit river, and within the limits of said city, which may be violating the provisions of this ordinance, and to order any person on board of, and having charge of said steamboat or vessel, either officer or seaman, to remove said steamboat or vessel, or otherwise to comply with this ordinance; and any person who shall neglect or refuse to obey said order, who shall obstruct, hinder, or resist said officer in going aboard of said steamboat or vessel, or who shall take off, or attempt to take off, said officer in said steamboat or vessel, when he has boarded the same in conformity to the powers herein vested in him, shall, upon conviction thereof, be punished by a fine of not less than fifty dollars, nor more than two hundred and fifty dollars, or by imprisonment not to exceed one year.

SEC. 8. Whenever the Marshal or any officer mentioned in this ordinance, shall receive a written or verbal complaint or information, or in any manner know of a violation of this ordinance, it shall be the duty of said Marshal or other officer forthwith to repair to the place where such violation has occurred or is occurring, and to exercise any and every power vested in him to enforce this ordinance, and to complain of the person or persons guilty of said violation; and if said Marshal or other officer shall refuse or neglect to comply with the provisions of this section, he shall be punished by a fine of twenty-five dollars, or by twenty days' imprisonment.

Marshal or other officer to visit the place on information of any violation of ordinance.

SEC. 9. This ordinance shall not be so construed as to prohibit vessels projecting in front of the foot of streets or public docks while discharging or receiving freight or passengers from or on an adjoining dock or wharf.

Construction of ordinance as to vessels loading, &c.

TITLE FOUR.

OF DRAINS AND SEWERS.

CHAPTER XXIII.

Relative to public and private Drains and Sewers.

SECTION 1. That no person or persons be permitted to connect any drain from his, her or their premises, with any public drain or sewer, now made or constructed, or hereafter to be made or constructed, in said city, nor with any private drain, whereby his, her or their premises will be drained into any public drain or sewer, except on previous application in writing to, and permission by, the Common Council, or Board of Sewer Commissioners, and the payment of the assessment hereinafter mentioned.

No lot to be drained without application to the Common Council and payment of assessment.

SEC. 2. All private drains to be hereafter made by individuals in any public street, lane or alley in said city, and connecting with any public drain or sewer, shall be of such size, dimensions and materials, and constructed and laid as directed by the Board of Sewer Commissioners, and shall enter such public drain or sewer under and according to the personal supervision and direction of their Engineer,

Council to determine the size of drains and to be entered under supervision of Engineer of Sewer Commissioners.

nor shall any person or persons enter any public drain or sewer at any other places than those designated and fixed for that purpose in the construction thereof.

Assessment for draining cellars.

SEC. 3. The amount which individuals using, or being benefitted by any public drain or sewer, shall pay for such use, is hereby fixed as follows, to wit: the sum of one dollar and fifty cents annually, for each cellar drained by box directly or indirectly into any public drain or sewer, which assessment shall be taken to include all other drainage of the premises to which said cellar especially belongs; and the sum of fifty cents annually for each lot or subdivision of lot being without a cellar, drained by box, as aforesaid, into any public drain or sewer; and such sums as may be fixed by the Common Council for all establishments requiring an unusual or extraordinary amount of drainage, drained as aforesaid, upon actual inspection of, and report thereon by the assessors.

When to be paid.

SEC. 4. That said assessment shall in all instances be paid when the city and school taxes are collected.

Persons using drain or sewer liable to assessment

SEC. 5. Any person whose premises are drained directly or indirectly, into any public drain or sewer, or any person using said premises thus drained, or for whose benefit or family the same is used, shall be liable to the payment therefor, and in addition said assessment shall become, and be a charge and lien on the premises thus drained, and be recovered, and the same proceedings had in every respect for the recovery thereof, as are provided for the recovery of other special assessments, and the corporation may also, at their option, stop such private drain, and prevent any person from draining his premises into any public drain or sewer, where such assessment shall not be paid in advance, on the second application, and said privilege shall not be restored unless on the payment of the tax and a forfeiture of double the amount of the assessment.

Assessment lien on lots.

How collected.

Drain may be cut off.

Penalty for injuring drain.

SEC. 6. Any person who shall remove any grate from the pool, over which it is placed, or in any way, directly or indirectly, injure any public drain or sewer, or any part thereof, shall, on conviction thereof before the Recorder's Court, be liable to a penalty for each offence, not exceeding one hundred dollars and costs.

Penalty for connecting with drains without permission.

SEC. 7. Any person who shall connect any drain from his premises with any public drain or sewer, or who shall drain his premises into any private drain which enters into any public drain or sewer, without first making the application, procuring the permission and paying the assessment, provided for in the first section of this chapter, shall, on conviction of each offence before the Recorder's Court, be liable to a penalty not exceeding one hundred dollars and costs; and any person who shall construct and lay any private drain, connecting with any public drain or sewer, or who shall enter any public drain or sewer, in any other manner except as is provided for in the second section of this chapter, shall be liable for each offence, on like conviction, to a penalty not exceeding one hundred dollars and costs; and any person who shall enter any public drain or sewer at any other place than is designated and fixed for that purpose in the construction thereof, shall be also liable to pay for each offence, on like conviction, a penalty not exceeding one hundred dollars and costs; and if any person shall drain his premises along the side of any public drain or sewer, he shall also be liable to pay a penalty not exceeding one hundred dollars and costs, on like conviction: *Provided*, That this section shall not be construed to extend to any case where a private drain has heretofore been laid down along the side of any public drain or sewer; but such private drain shall not be repaired by any person without having received from the Common Council, or some authorized officer of said city, a certificate that such repair will not endanger the safety and preservation of any public drain or sewer along the side thereof.

How to enter drains.

Drain not to be placed by public drain.

SEC. 8. That no person be permitted to connect any drain from his premises with the grand sewer, nor enter the same between the first day of December and the first day of April in each year, and any person offending against this section, shall, on conviction of such offence before the Recorder's Court, be liable to pay a fine of one hundred dollars and costs.

When sewers may be entered.

SEC. 9. That all drains now made and constructed, or which shall hereafter be made and constructed by the corporation, shall be deemed to be public drains or sewers within the purview of this chapter; and all sums of money received under the provisions of this chapter shall be stated and kept in a separate account, and are hereby specifically pledged and appropriated to the following uses and objects, and no other, to wit: 1st, to defray the expense of indispensable repairs of existing sewers; 2d, to defray the cost of additional public sewers and their repairs; 3d, to apply on the interest of the city debt ac-

What drains are public.

How sewer assessments to be appropriated.

TITLE IV. CHAPTER 23.

cruing on account of the cost of construction and maintenance of such sewers.

How sewer assessments may be collected.

SEC. 10. The assessment provided for in this chapter shall be collected in the manner prescribed by the chapter "relating to the collection of special assessments," the provisions of which are made applicable hereto, except that the time of the warrants and provision of percentage shall be made to correspond with the terms of the warrants and the provisions for percentage in the collection of the city and school taxes.

Private Drains.

Certain portion of expense to be paid before connection with drains.

SEC. 11. That no person be permitted to connect any drain from his, her or their premises with any drain or sewer made by one or more individuals in any street, lane or alley as aforesaid, unless on payment to the proprietors of such drain or sewer of a rateable proportion of the expense of making the same, the amount to be ascertained and determined by the Marshal or Surveyor, with the right of appeal to the Common Council; nor shall any person make or construct a sink, drain or sewer leading into any other drain or sewer, without putting a sufficient strainer at the head of it, under a penalty not exceeding ten dollars and costs, for each offence.

How expense of repairs ascertained.

SEC. 12. Every person having any drain from his, her or their premises, that shall be connected with any drain or sewer now made, or that shall hereafter be made as aforesaid, shall pay a rateable proportion of all expenses necessary for maintaining and keeping such drains or sewers in repair, such proportion to be ascertained and determined in the manner provided for in the foregoing section, and if any person shall neglect to pay the same, when so ascertained, such person shall forfeit and pay the sum of two dollars and costs, for every week during which the same shall remain unpaid.

Penalty.

Marshal to notify persons to repair.

SEC. 13. In all cases where drains or sewers shall be obstructed so as to become, in the opinion of the Marshal, a nuisance, it shall be his duty to give notice to the persons using the same, to repair such drains or sewers, and if the same be not forthwith repaired, it shall be the duty of the Marshal to cause the necessary repairs to be made, and to charge the said persons with a rateable proportion of the expense incurred, including a reasonable allowance to the Marshal for his own services, subject to an appeal to the Common Council, as is provided in the tenth section; and all such appeals shall be made within the time in which such person is required to pay the sums above required; and if any person shall refuse or neglect to pay their proportion of the charges for the space of ten days after notice, he or they shall be liable, upon conviction before the Recorder's Court, to pay a fine not exceeding fifty dollars, and with costs of suit.

Proceedings in case of neglect.

SEC. 14. No connection with public or private sewers or drains shall be made under the provisions of this chapter, until the Surveyor shall have designated the grade therefor, under the penalty of twenty dollars.

No connection to be made until Surveyor shall have ascertained the grade.

CHAPTER XXIV.

Relative to Lateral Sewers or Drains.

SECTION 1. That the Common Council may, by resolution, direct the construction, cleansing or repair of lateral sewers or drains through or in any streets or alleys, or the construction, cleansing or repairs of drains from any house, yard or lot, when, in their opinion, the same shall be necessary. Such drains or sewers to be built of such materials as the said Common Council shall direct, and be laid or constructed in such direction, of such size and width, such descent, and with such strainers or grates as said Common Council shall direct.

Com. Coun. may order lateral sewers to be built, &c.

SEC. 2. Whenever the Common Council shall direct, as aforesaid, the construction, cleansing or repair of any lateral sewer or drain, as provided for in section one, it shall be the duty of the City Surveyor to assess the expense of constructing, cleansing or repairing the same, in a rateable proportion to the owners or occupants of all land or lots adjoining said street or alley; or to the owner or occupant of the land or lot through which such drain shall run.

City Surveyor to assess the expense of building, repairing, &c

SEC. 3. The City Clerk shall cause the assessment rolls to be delivered to the City Treasurer, who shall retain them in his office for the space of five days, from and after the date of such delivery; and during said period, any person assessed therein may pay the amount of his, or her assessment to the City Treasurer. Upon the expiration of the said period of five days, it shall be the duty of the City Treasurer to deliver the said assessment rolls, or a certified copy thereof, adding thereto all costs incurred in the premises, to the Controller, who shall issue a warrant under his hand and the seal of the

City Treasu'r to retain rolls 5 days in his office and receive pay.

Controller to issue warrant for collection.

TITLE IV. CHAPTER 24.

city, directed to the City Collector of said city, with a command to levy and collect all sums or assessments then remaining unpaid, with the costs and charges thereon, and five cents on the dollar for his services, by distress and sale of the goods and chattels of the person against whom said assessment has been made, or those who may be liable to pay the same; and further, commanding the City Collector to make returns to the Common Council within five days thereafter.

Collector to make return within 5 days

Collector in case of neglect and refusal, to make a levy and sale at public auction.

SEC. 4. Upon receiving the assessment roll, or a copy thereof, and warrant, it shall be the duty of the City Collector to proceed to demand and collect the several sums mentioned therein, and if any person shall neglect or refuse to pay the same, then, if he can find any goods or chattels of the person liable therefor, he shall levy thereon, and shall proceed to sell such goods and chattels at public auction, to the highest bidder, and shall render the surplus, (if any,) after deducting costs and charges, of such distress and sale, to the person entitled thereto.

Only persons named in roll to make connections except by permission of C. Council.

SEC. 5. No parties, except those embraced in the said assessment roll, shall connect with any such lateral sewer or drain, without permission of the Common Council, and without payment to the City Treasurer of such sum or sums as the City Surveyor shall decide it to be right and proper for them to pay; and any person or persons who shall violate this section, shall be prosecuted before the Recorder's Court, and fined not to exceed ten dollars and costs of prosecution, and the amount so decided upon by the Surveyor, shall also be recovered before said Court.

Penalty.

Lots sufficiently drained to be exempt.

SEC. 6. Whenever any lot or premises subject to assessment, under and by virtue of this ordinance, shall, in the opinion of the Common Council, be already sufficiently drained by a private drain or sewer, said lot or premises shall not be assessed for any of the purposes for which an assessment is provided by this ordinance: *Proded always*, That it shall be the duty of the owner or occupant of said lot or premises to inform the Common Council of the fact that said lot or premises are so drained in the manner hereinafter provided.

Proviso.

City Clerk to publish notice of assessment 5 days.

SEC. 7. Whenever an assessment shall be ordered to be made under this ordinance, it shall be the duty of the City Clerk of said city to publish a notice for five days in the daily newspaper published by the contractor to do the printing of the city, which said notice shall state the fact that said assessment has been ordered by the Common Council, the purposes for which it has been ordered, and that said Common Council will, at their next regular meeting, after the expiration of said five days, permit any person whose lot or premises are liable to be included in said assessment, to show to said Council that said lot or premises are drained in the manner set forth in the preceding section.

City Surveyor to omit lots in certain cases.

SEC. 8. If the Common Council resolve that said lot or premises are sufficiently drained by a private drain or sewer, the City Surveyor shall omit said lot or premises from said assessment.

Other ordinances repealed.

SEC. 9. All ordinances or parts of ordinances of the Revised Ordinances of 1855, in contravention of this ordinance, are hereby repealed.

To take effect forthwith.

SEC. 10. This ordinance shall take effect and be in force from and after its passage.

CHAPTER XXV.

To define the Powers and Duties of the Board of Sewer Commissioners.

Board to elect President annually.

SECTION 1. The Board of Sewer Commissioners shall annually, dating from the time of their organization, elect one of their number President.

Engineer to act as Secretary; his duties and salary.

SEC. 2. The Engineer of Sewers shall act as Secretary of said Board, and shall, under the direction of said Board, superintend the construction and repairs of all public sewers or drains, and pools, and sewers and drains built by special assessments. His salary shall be fixed by resolution of the Common Council.

Board may appoint inspectors.

SEC. 3. Said Board, when specially authorized by resolution of the Common Council, may appoint such inspectors of work and other agents as may be required for carrying out the work committed to their charge by the charter and by this ordinance; which inspectors and agents shall receive such compensation for their services as the Common Council may allow or prescribe.

General supervision of sewers.

SEC. 4. Said Board shall have the supervision of the construction of all sewers hereafter to be built, whether they be built at the expense of the city or by special assessment upon the individuals to be

TITLE IV. CHAPTER 25.

benefitted thereby, and of all repairs of sewers and pools hereafter to be performed, and are hereby fully authorized and empowered to enforce, or otherwise carry out all contracts for the building or repairing of sewers, drains and pools within said city.

Board to submit plans to Council and report.

SEC. 5. Said Board shall, as soon as may be, submit to the Common Council "a plan for constructing sewers and drains for the whole city, having reference, however, to the sewers and drains already constructed or in process of construction," and shall, at the first meeting of the Common Council in February of each year, report to said Common Council what public sewers and drains they deem necessary to build in that year, and shall accompany the report with an estimate of the cost of each and all of said sewers, and of all the probable expenses of the construction of public sewers during the year then next ensuing.

Council to decide on sewers to be built, &c.

SEC. 6. The Common Council shall decide what public sewers and drains shall be built in said year, and shall, through the City Clerk, notify said Board of their decision; and said Board shall, without delay, report to said Common Council an estimate of the cost of any sewer or drain which the Common Council shall thus order to be built, and which was not embraced in the estimate provided for in the foregoing section; and shall proceed to advertise for proposals to build all the sewers and drains ordered to be built by the Common Council, under such specifications and forms as the said Board may deem necessary; which advertisement shall be published at least ten days in the newspaper published by the contractor to do the city printing, and shall state the time when and place where said proposals shall be received and opened; and shall require each party making a proposal to accompany the same with a statement in writing signed by at least two persons, who agree thereby to become sureties in an amount at least double the estimated cost of the work proposed to be performed, for the faithful performance of said work.

Board to advertise.

Proposals where opened.

SEC. 7. Said proposals shall be received and opened by said Board publicly in the office of the City Controller, and in his presence, and a copy of each proposal shall be recorded by the said City Controller, and also by the Secretary of said Board.

Board to examine proposals.

SEC. 8. When said proposals shall have been received and opened as aforesaid, said Board, together with the City Controller, shall proceed to examine the same, and determine who are the lowest responsible bidders, possessing the qualifications required by the charter of said city; whereupon the Controller shall communicate their determination, together with all said proposals, to the Common Council, who shall consider said proposals and communication, and award the contract proposed to be performed to the lowest responsible qualified bidder, and shall return said proposals and communicate their decision to said Board. The said Board shall transmit the proper specifications of the work to be performed to the City Attorney, who shall draw a contract for the performance of said work in accordance with said specifications and of the charter and ordinances of said city, which said contract shall be signed on the part of the city by said Board, and attested under the corporate seal by the City Clerk; and shall, when executed, be placed in the keeping of said Board, whose duty it shall be to see that the contractor or contractors shall comply therewith.

Controller to make statement to Council.

Attorney to draw contract.

To be attested by Clerk.

SEC. 9. Said Board shall certify to the amount due upon all contracts, and for all materials furnished and labor performed in building or repairing sewers and pools, and all bills and accounts thus certified for amounts so due shall be audited by the Controller, and presented by him to the Council, in the same manner as other bills and accounts against said city.

Board to certify to all accounts for work, &c.

SEC. 10. Said Board shall keep, or cause to be kept, an accurate record of all their proceedings, which shall at all times be subject to the examination and inspection of any citizen of said city, and shall, once in each year, or oftener, if required, submit to said Common Council a report of all their proceedings, with the names of their employees, and the total expenses of the construction and repairs of sewers and pools, since the last report, and such other information as they may deem necessary or as said Council may require.

To keep record of proceedings and submit the same yearly to Council.

SEC. 11. Said Board shall not lay down or construct any sewer or pool in said city, or purchase any materials, or enter into any contract, except as provided in this ordinance; and except in case of any unexpected casualty or damage to the sewers or pools of said city, in which case said Board may cause the same to be repaired to the amount of not exceeding two hundred dollars, and shall report their proceedings therein, and the necessity therefor, to the next regular meeting of the Common Council.

In certain cases may order work to the amount of $200.

SEC. 12. No connection shall be made with any public sewer or

TITLE V. CHAPTER 26.

Board to give permit for connecting with sewers.

drain, except with the permission of said Board, and under the direction of the Engineer, who shall, at least once in each month, notify the City Assessor of all such connections, made since the last notice; and any person connecting with any public sewer without such permission, shall be fined not to exceed one hundred dollars, or imprisoned three months, or both, in the discretion of the court.

City Clerk to supply stationery.

SEC. 13. The City Clerk shall supply the said Board with all necessary stationery.

SEC. 14. This ordinance shall take effect and be in force from and after its passage.

TITLE FIVE.

OF MARKETS AND SALES.

CHAPTER XXVI.

Relative to Public Markets.

Markets held where Council shall designate.

SECTION 1. All public markets in the city of Detroit shall be held in such places as the Common Council shall from time to time designate and license, and in no other.

Mayor to issue licenses to sell fresh meat.

SEC. 2. The Mayor shall, from time to time, issue licenses to so many and such persons as the Common Council may direct, to sell fresh meat in such places within the limits of the city, as may be designated in such license, but not elsewhere.

Said licenses shall expire first Monday in April, after they are granted.

SEC. 3. All licenses so issued shall expire and cease on the first Monday of April after the granting thereof, unless sooner revoked by the Common Council, and shall be renewed by the Mayor, under the direction of the Common Council, on application.

Fifty dollars to be paid for licenses.

SEC. 4. For each license issued as aforesaid, the sum of fifty dollars shall be paid or secured on the granting of the same, and a like sum for the renewal of the same.

Shops where fresh meat and fish are

SEC. 5. All shops, cellars, stalls and other places, within the limits of the city, where fresh meat and fish are sold, shall be under the supervision of the Clerk of the City Hall market, and subject to all the regulations which are established by law, for the cleanliness and good government of the public markets.

Sold to be under the supervision of the Clerk of the Market

SEC. 6. No person shall use or occupy, or cause to be used or occupied, any stall or stalls in the public market house belonging to the Corporation, unless he shall have paid for, or secured the payment for the same, as hereinafter provided, and when so paid, or the payment thereof secured, such person shall keep such stall or stalls well supplied with good and wholesome meat, to be sold therein.

How stalls in markets to be used and occupied.

SEC. 7. The Common Council shall, from time to time, determine the rent of all stalls in the public markets, and the said stalls shall be rented at the rate so determined, either by the year or for a term of years, (provided said term shall not exceed three years in all,) under the direction of the Controller and Committee on Markets, whose duty it shall be to let all stalls which are or are about to become vacant, to responsible parties, at the rent so determined by the Council: *Provided, always*, That persons renting stalls, who are not in arrears for the rent thereof, shall, upon the expiration of their terms, have the privilege of renting the same stalls for a further term, at the rate of rent fixed for the same by the Common Council, at the expiration of their terms.

Common Council to determine the rents of stalls, and stalls to be rented under the direction of Controller and Com'itee on Markets.

SEC. 8. Any person who shall rent a stall under the provisions of the preceding section, shall pay the first quarter's rent thereof, in advance, to the Treasurer, and shall give to the City adequate security, to be approved by, and filed with the Treasurer, for the payment of the rent of said stalls quarterly, in advance, during the term for which he has rented the same; and shall further enter into a written agreement, to be signed by him and by the Treasurer, stating the term for, the price at, and the conditions on which said stall is rented.

One fourth of rent to be paid in advance and the rest secured.

SEC. 9. The market houses belonging to the Corporation shall be kept open every day (Sundays excepted,) from daylight till the hour from time to time fixed by resolution of the Common Council, and not otherwise: *Provided*, The provisions of this section shall not apply to markets other than belonging to the Corporation.

When markets shall be kept open.

SEC. 10. It shall not be lawful for any person or persons to sell or expose for sale any fresh meat, (poultry and venison excepted,) in any quantity, at any time, or in any building, or street, or other place

Meats not to be sold except in market house or places designated by Council.

TITLE V. CHAPTER 26.

whatever within the limits of this city, excepting in the stalls in the respective market houses rented from the Corporation, according to existing regulations, and such other places as may be designated by the Common Council, as hereinbefore provided: *Provided*, That nothing herein contained shall prevent any person or persons from selling or exposing for sale in the streets, in the immediate vicinity of the public markets, or elsewhere, fresh meat by the carcass or quarter, according to the provisions of the next succeeding chapter of these ordinances, relative to sale of fresh meat by the quarter, within the bounds of the city of Detroit.

Persons occupying stalls to keep a tub for offal, and to remove the offal one hour after market closes

SEC. 11. Every person occupying a stall in any of the public markets, shall procure and place in such markets a suitable cask or tub, in which he shall deposit, or cause to be deposited, the offals of all slaughtered animals, brought or caused to be brought by him, therein, and such person shall within one hour after the closing of the market house, remove, or cause to be removed therefrom, all such offals as aforesoid; but no person shall bring, or cause to be brought into any public market house, any hides or skins of slaughtered animals, except on calves, sheep, lambs or hogs.

Certain hides not to be brought to markets.

When sales may be out of market hours.

SEC. 12. If any person who may have rented a stall from the Corporation, as aforesaid, shall, within the ordinary hours of business, make application to the Clerk of the City Hall market for the privilege of selling meat after the time the market house is required to be closed, and can satisfy the Clerk that it is for the sole purpose of supplying some boat or vessel about to sail from said city, or traveler about to leave the city in the cars, but in no other, the Clerk may grant such privilege.

All provisions offered shall be sound; if not may be seized and venders punished.

SEC. 13. All provisions opened or exposed for sale in said markets shall be sound and wholesome, and of pure and good quality, and if otherwise, shall be seized, and the sellers or manufacturers thereof, and each and every person engaged in such manufacture, shall be liable for each offence, to a penalty not exceeding one hundred dollars; and all weights and measures used in said markets shall be in conformity with the standard weights and measures regulated by the laws of this State; and any person who shall within the limits of said city, sell, or offer to sell, or exhibit for sale, any article which shall be deficient in the weight or measure for which he sells the same, or offers or exhibits the same for sale, shall, upon conviction before the Recorder's Court, forfeit a penalty of not more than one hundred dollars and costs of prosecution.

Markets to be kept clean and clear of obstructions.

SEC. 14. Said markets, and a space of twenty feet without them and adjacent thereto on every side, shall be kept clear during market hours, of carts, wagons, carriages, wheelbarrows and other vehicles, and of all animals and other obstructions whatsoever, and also of all offals and offensive substances of every kind; and all stalls and meat blocks and benches shall be within the said market houses and not elsewhere, and shall be kept clean: *Provided, however*, That this section shall not be so construed as to prevent the ordinary travel of the highway.

Bad conduct prohibited in markets.

SEC. 15. That within the space of twenty feet aforesaid, and within said market houses, there shall not be any lewd, lascivious or disorderly conduct, nor loud or boisterous noises made, nor any profane or vulgar language used, nor any act done or committed tending to a breach of the public peace, or to disturb the decorum of the place.

Duty of Clerk of market to enforce the provisions of this chapter in Recorder's Court.

SEC. 16. It will be the duty of the Clerk of the City Hall market, and he is hereby authorized and empowered to attend all said markets and enforce the due execution of the provisions of this chapter, and make complaint to the Recorder's Court, of each and every infringement of this chapter, and also to remove from the said markets all offensive substances or offals, and all obstructions before mentioned.

Vegetable market designated.

SEC. 17. That the ground enclosed by a railing, beginning at the east end of the City Hall, and extending along Michigan Grand avenue to Randolph street, and all other yards, grounds or enclosures that have been or may hereafter be designated by said Common Council as places for holding vegetable markets, be, and the same are hereby declared public markets, and that the provisions of this chapter for the prevention of disorderly conduct, shall apply to said vegetable markets, and to a place twenty feet without them, and to the adjacent streets on every side.

What may be sold in vegetable market.

SEC. 18. All fresh fish, poultry, eggs, butter, fruits or vegetables of any kind, may be sold within the limits prescribed in the next preceding section of this chapter, or any grounds that have been or may hereafter be designated as vegetable markets, and on no other public grounds or streets in said city during the hours the market

TITLE V. CHAPTER 27.

houses are required to be kept open: *Provided*, That nothing herein contained shall prevent the sale of the above articles from wagons within the immediate vicinity of said vegetable markets.

How vegetables, &c., exposed; if unsound, Clerk shall order them removed.

SEC. 19. All provisions or vegetables offered for sale at any of the public markets, shall be placed on stands elevated from the ground, in such a manner, and shall remain stationed at such place or places as the Clerk of the respective markets shall direct, and if any of such provisions or vegetables shall be deemed by such Clerk to be unwholesome or unfit to be consumed or used, he shall order owners thereof to remove the same immediately from the public markets; and if such owner shall neglect or refuse to remove such provisions or vegetables as aforesaid, it shall be the duty of said Clerk to remove the same without delay.

No public market house to be used save for sale of meat.

SEC. 20. No person shall use or occupy any public market house, or any part thereof, but for the sale of meat, or cutting, or salting the same, except when permission shall have been obtained for that purpose, as hereinafter provided.

Hucksters, forestallers and grocers prohibited from occupying certain places in vegetable market.

SEC. 21. It shall not be lawful for any huckster, forestaller, grocer, or other person, to occupy the spaces on either side of the platform extending back from the rear of the City Hall vegetable market, for the purpose of vending any meats, butter, vegetables, fruits or other articles of merchandise previously purchased by them.

Penalty for violations.

SEC. 22. If any person shall violate any of the provisions of this chapter, he or she shall, on conviction before the Recorder's Court, for every such offence, be subject to pay a fine not exceeding one hundred dollars and costs of prosecution.

CHAPTER XXVII.

Relative to Forestalling.

Forestalling defined, prohibited and how punished.

SECTION 1. It shall not be lawful for any person who follows the business of huckster, forestaller, grocer or seller of any articles of provision at second hand, to purchase or offer to purchase, either personally or by his or her agent, within the limits of said city, during the hours the public markets are required to be kept open each day, any fresh venison, fresh fish, poultry, game of any kind, eggs, butter, fruit, or vegetables of any kind, from any person bringing or having brought the same to said city for sale or barter. And the possession of any such article by any such huckster, forestaller, grocer, or other seller thereof, which may have been previously in the possession of any farmer or other person, within the limits of the said city, during the hours aforesaid, shall be deemed *prima facie* evidence of a violation of this ordinance. Any person violating the provisions of this ordinance shall be subject to a fine of not more than fifty dollars and costs of prosecution, to be recovered in the Recorder's Court.

CHAPTER XXVIII.

Relative to the Sale of Meat by the Quarter.

Persons may be licensed to sell meat by quarter.

SECTION 1. The Common Council in session, or the Mayor in vacation, may hereafter license any person who is a resident of the State of Michigan, and of the age of twenty-one years, to buy and sell meat by the carcass or quarter, from shops, wagons, carts or other vehicles within the limits of the city of Detroit, upon the payment at the rate of one hundred dollars per annum, for each and every shop, wagon, cart or other uehicle to be used for that purpose, and that no license be granted for a less term than three months.

To give bonds.

SEC. 2. Every person so applying for such license, shall first execute a bond to be approved by the Council, in the penal sum of two hundred dollars, conditioned that he will at no time offer for sale, or suffer to be offered for sale, any unwholesome meats of any kind or description, and that he will occupy such place or stand, in the vicinity of the market, or elsewhere, as shall be assigned to him by the Common Council, and that he will preserve order about his shop or vehicle, while occupying such stand.

No person to sell by the quarter unless licensed.

Penalty.

SEC. 3. No person, unless licensed as hereinbefore provided, shall hereafter peddle, sell, or offer for sale, from any shop, wagon, cart or other vehicle used for that purpose, in or about the markets of said city, or in any of the streets thereof, any beef, pork, mutton, or other meats by the carcass or quarter, under a penalty not exceeding fifty dollars for every such offence, to be recovered in the Recorder's Court, with the costs of prosecution: *Provided*, That it shall not be considered a violation of the provisions of this section for drovers or others to sell any such meat as aforesaid, either by the carcass or the quarter, to any or either of the regular butchers of the city occupying stalls rented of the city of Detroit, in either of the public markets of said city.

Farmers not prohibited from selling by the quarter, when.

SEC. 4. The foregoing provisions shall not be so construed as to apply to any farmer who shall offer for sale any meat which may have been fatted and killed by him; but shall be applied only to such persons as may offer such articles for sale—the same having been previously purchased by them for that purpose; and for the purpose of a conviction under this chapter, the possession of such articles by such party shall be deemed *prima facie* evidence of such purchase.

Drovers not to sell by the quarter.

SEC. 6. Nothing in this chapter contained shall be construed to authorize any person following the business of a drover for a livelihood, to sell meat by the quarter, unless he shall be licensed under this chapter.

CHAPTER XXIX.

Relative to the Sale of Woodcock, &c.

When woodcock, partridges, &c., shall not be sold.

SECTION 1. It shall not be lawful for any person to offer for sale, or sell within the limits of the city of Detroit, or bring into the city for the purpose of selling the same, or for any other purpose, any woodcocks killed between the first day of February and the first day of July in each year, or any quails, partridges or pheasants killed between the first day of March and the first day of October, in each year.

Penalty.

SEC. 2. Any person who shall expose for sale, or sell, or have in his possession for the purpose of selling the same, or for any other purpose, within the limits of said city, any woodcocks, quails, partridges or pheasants, killed within the periods specified in the first section of this chapter, shall forfeit and pay the sum of fifty cents for each woodcock, quail, partridge or pheasant, to be recovered in an action of debt before the Recorder's Court of said city, one half of which sum shall be paid upon recovery, to the Treasurer of the city of Detroit, and one half to the person who shall sue and prosecute therefor.

CHAPTER XXX.

Relative to the Sale of Hay and Straw.

SECTION 1. It shall be the duty of the Weighmasters, severally, well and truly to weigh any cart, wagon, or sled load of hay, when applied to by any person desiring the same, and make such reduction from the weight of said hay as to him may seem reasonable and just, by reason of said hay being damp, wet or not well cured, and deliver to the person so applying a certificate thereof, for which he may demand and receive of such applicant twenty five cents. Weigh master to weigh hay and issue certificate

SEC. 2. No person or persons shall sell or offer for sale any hay in said city, by the cart, wagon or sled load, unless the same shall have been first weighed in the manner above prescribed, and as soon as conveniently may be, after unloading said hay, the cart, wagon, sled, or other vehicle bearing the same, with all things and apparatus belonging thereto, at the time of weighing said hay, shall also be weighed; and the seller shall deliver unto the buyer the certificate given by the weighmaster, at the time of demanding payment for the hay so sold. No hay to be sold unless first weighed

SEC. 3. The purchaser or purchasers of any hay which shall have been weighed in the manner above directed, may require and cause the same, as well as the cart, wagon, sled or other vehicle, bearing the same, to be weighed at his own expense, and the seller of such hay shall not refuse to let the same be so weighed. Purchaser may have hay weighed.

SEC. 4. All carts, wagons, sleds or other vehicles, loaded with hay intended for sale, shall stand at, or adjoining the hay scales, in regular order, one after the other, and in such manner as not to obstruct the centre of any street, and so as to leave access to any house or other building thereon open and unobstructed. How hay carts or other vehicles to stand.

SEC. 5. All the foregoing provisions of this chapter shall apply relative to any straw sold or offered for sale in said city, except straw made up into bundles and sold by the bundle. Provisions of this chapter applied to straw.

SEC. 6. Any person offending against the provisions of this chapter, shall be liable to a fine not exceeding fifty dollars and costs of prosecution for each offence. Penalty.

TITLE V. CHAPTER 31.

CHAPTER XXXI.

Relative to Unwholesome Liquors and Provisions.

No person shall sell diseased or unwholesome flesh, bread or drink.

SECTION 1. No butcher or other person shall sell or offer to sell within the limits of the city of Detroit, the flesh of any animal dying otherwise than by slaughter, nor the flesh of any animal slaughtered when diseased, nor any contagious or unwholesome flesh of any description whatsoever, nor any provisions of any description, except such as are sound, and of pure and wholesome quality; and no baker, brewer, distiller or other person, shall sell, or offer, or expose to sale, any unwholesome bread or other provisions, drink or liquors whatever; and any person offending in the premises shall, on conviction thereof before the Recorder's Court, be fined in a sum not exceeding five hundred dollars, and the costs of prosecution, and be liable to be excluded from the public markets of this city, and from the exercise of his business, notwithstanding such person may have rented a stall or stalls in one or more markets, or paid a license; and it shall at all times be the duty of all the constables and other officers of this city to take notice of, and report all infractions of this chapter.

Penalty.

Unsound sausages.

SEC. 2. Any person who shall sell or offer for sale, or who shall aid in effecting any sale, or in the manufacture or preparation of sausages or other provisions, composed of bad, impure, decayed or unsound ingredients, shall be liable to the penalties in the foregoing section.

CHAPTER XXXII.

Relative to Sale of Goods at Auction.

No goods to be sold in streets save by process of law.

SECTION 1. No goods, wares, merchandise or other property, personal or real, shall be sold, or exposed for sale in any street or alley, or on any sidewalk, wharf or pier in the city of Detroit, or at the door or window of any store or dwelling in said city, by any auctioneer or other person, except a Marshal, Master in Chancery, Coroner, Sheriff or Collector, by virtue of an execution or other authority, vested in him by law, except such articles as are permitted to be sold by the second section of this chapter.

SEC. 2. It shall and may be lawful for any auctioneer, or other person not prohibited by law, to sell or expose for sale, at auction or vendue, on any wharf, or in any street of said city, all spirituous, vinous and malt liquors, cider and other liquors, in casks which shall contain not less than thirty gallons, ship furniture and tackle, carriages, farming utensils, household furniture, animals of every description, and all other goods, wares or merchandise, in packages or parcels, the size of which shall be equal to the bulk of one barrel, or which shall weigh one hundred pounds: *Provided*, The selling or exposing to sale such articles does not encumber the sidewalks or obstruct the streets, so that persons, horses or carriages cannot conveniently pass.

What may be sold in the streets.

SEC. 3. No bell man, crier, or other means of attracting the attention of passengers, shall be used or employed by any auctioneer or other person, for the purpose of collecting bidders at the sale or auction of any property.

Bell men prohibited.

SEC. 4. Any person or persons who shall violate any of the provisions of this chapter, shall, on conviction thereof, before the Recorder's Court of the city of Detroit, be subject to a fine not exceeding fifty dollars and costs of prosecution.

Penalty.

SEC. 5, It shall not be lawful for any person to vend or sell at public auction or vendue, any horse or cattle in any of the public streets of the city of Detroit, south of Campus Martius; and any person offending in the premises shall, for every offence, on conviction thereof before the Recorder's Court of said city, pay a fine not exceeding one hundred dollars and costs of prosecution.

Not lawful to sell cattle in certain parts of city.

SEC. 6. It shall be the duty of the Marshal of said city to cause this chapter strictly to be carried into effect.

Duty of Marshal.

CHAPTER XXXIII.

Relative to the Manufacture and Sale of Bread.

SECTION 1. It shall not be lawful for any person to use or carry on the trade or business of a baker, either in person or by employing any other person to use or carry on the said trade or business, under his or her direction, or for his or her profit or benefit, within said city, without having obtained from the Common Council a permit for that pupose, under a penalty not exceeding fifty dollars.

Bakers to obtain permits.

TITLE V. CHAPTER 33.

How obtained.

SEC. 2. Every person desirous to use or carry on said trade or business, shall make application in writing to the Common Council, setting forth the street and house in which he or she intends to carry on said trade or business, and shall accompany such application with a recommendation signed by at least twelve respectable householders of said city, certifying that such person is qualified to carry on said business, and that he or she is of good fame and correct and orderly deportment and behavior.

Clerk to deliver permit if granted.

SEC. 3. If the Common Council shall grant such application, the Clerk shall deliver such person a permit for the purpose aforesaid, for which he shall be entitled to receive from such person the sum of twenty-five cents; and the said permit shall be in force till the second Tuesday in March then next ensuing.

Bread to be made of good flour.

SEC. 4. All bread manufactured by the bakers of this city for sale, shall be made of good and wholesome flour or meal into loaves of one pound and two pounds avoirdupois weight, and every loaf of such bread shall be marked with the numbers indicating the weight of such loaf, and also with the initial letters of the name of the baker thereof; and if any baker or other person shall offer or expose for sale any bread made of unwholesome materials, or any bread not so marked, except as aforesaid, every such baker or other person so offending shall forfeit and pay for each loaf, a sum not exceeding twenty-five dollars.

Penalty for selling bread under weight

SEC. 5. If any baker shall make for sale, or shall sell or expose for sale any bread that shall be deficient in weight, according to the requisitions prescribed in the preceding section of this chapter, he shall forfeit and pay for every such offence the sum of ten cents for every ounce that such bread shall be deficient in weight: *Provided, always,* That such deficiency in the weight of such bread shall be ascertained by the inspector of bread, by weighing or causing the same to be weighed in his presence, within eight hours after the same shall have been baked, sold or exposed for sale: *And provided, further,* That whenever any allowance in the weight shall be claimed on account of any bread having been baked, sold or exposed for sale more than eight hours as aforesaid, the burden of proof in respect to the time when the same shall have been baked, sold or exposed for sale, shall devolve upon the defendant or baker of such bread.

SEC. 6. The City Marshal shall, ex-officio, be inspector of bread, and it shall be his duty, and he is hereby authorized and required from time to time, and not less than once in each month, at all seasonable hours, to enter into, and inspect and examine every baker's shop, storehouse or other building where any bread is or shall be baked, stored or deposited, or offered for sale, and to inspect and examine all bread found therein, and also to stop, detain and examine in any part of the said city, any person or persons, wagons or other carriages carrying any loaf of bread, and weigh the same, and determine whether the same are in violation of the true intent and meaning of this chapter; and if the said inspector shall find any bread not conformable to the directions herein contained, or any part of them, he shall make complaint thereof for the purpose of having such person prosecuted according to law.

Marshal to be bread Inspector.

SEC. 7. Any person or persons, who may obstruct, or in any manner impede or wilfully delay any person legally qualified, in the execution of his duties under this act, either by refusing to him or delaying his entrance or admission into any of the places above mentioned, or by refusing or omitting to stop their wagon or carriage as aforesaid, or in any other manner whatsoever, so that the due execution of this act or any part of it may be impeded or obstructed, every such person shall, for every such offence, on conviction thereof before the Recorder's Court, forfeit and pay a sum not exceeding fifty dollars and costs of prosecution, and further, his, her or their license as a baker, if any has been granted to such person, shall be forfeited.

Penalty for obstructing Marshal inspecting.

CHAPTER XXXIV.

Powers and Duties of Clerks of Markets.

SECTION 1. There shall be one Clerk of Markets in and for the city of Detroit, and as many more as the Common Council shall by previous resolution prescribe.

Clerks of Market.

SEC. 2. It shall be the duty of each Clerk of Markets to open and close the market under his charge at the hours fixed therefor by the Common Council; to preserve the order and cleanliness of said market, to enforce all regulations, orders and ordinances of the Common Council relative thereto, and to complain of all persons guilty

Duties of

TITLE V. CHAPTER 34.

of a violation of any of said ordinances or of this ordinance. He shall have power, and it is hereby made his duty, to arrest and eject from said market any persons who create a disturbance, fight, quarrel, swear, or in any manner disturb the peace of the same, to order any person standing in the doorways of said market, or encumbering or obstructing the passages of said market, to move on, and he shall arrest any person who shall disregard or disobey said order; and said person so disobeying shall, on conviction, be punished by a fine not to exceed twenty-five dollars, or by imprisonment not to exceed thirty days.

Powers of

Penalty.

Duty of clerk to examine all articles for sale.

SEC. 3. It shall be the duty of each Clerk to examine all articles in the market, which he may suspect to be unwholesome or stale, or blown, plaited, raised or stuffed meat, or measly pork, or flesh of animals dead by accident or disease, or known or suspected to be diseased at the time of killing the same, or which by reason of its age is prohibited to be sold by the ordinances. And if any person shall hinder, obstruct or molest said Clerk in the performance of this duty, said person shall be punished by fifty dollars' fine, or by twenty-five days' imprisonment for each and every offence. And it shall be the duty of said Clerk to see that no animal or game of any kind shall be exposed for sale in said market at the seasons of the year when it is unlawful to kill the same, under the statutes of the State of Michigan.

Penalty for obstructing clerk.

Clerk to set a place for selling garden produce, &c.

SEC. 4. It shall be the duty of each Clerk to assign or set apart portions of the space included in the limits of his market, for the purpose of exposing for sale and selling garden produce; and if any person shall expose for sale or sell any garden produce in any other place in said market than that so assigned, said person shall be punished by five dollars' fine, or two days' imprisonment for each and every offence.

Penalty.

Clerk to order removal of vehicles, &c.

SEC. 5. It shall be the duty of each Clerk to give directions respecting the arrangement or removal of any article, vehicle, cart, wagon, box, basket or other thing in his market, or the streets adjoining thereto, and any person who shall neglect or refuse to obey said directions shall be punished by a fine of five dollars, or by two days' imprisonment.

SEC. 6. In case of the refusal or neglect to obey said directions, it shall be lawful for, and shall be the duty of said Clerk of any market, forthwith to remove, or cause to be removed, such article, cart or vehicle, wagon, box, basket, or other thing directed to be removed, to such place as he shall have previously directed, or to such other place as he shall think proper within said market.

Clerk to remove vehicles, &c., on refusal of owners to do so.

SEC. 7. That each clerk shall have power to suspend any person having a stated stall or stand in any public market, or occupying any part of said market, whether said person be a licensed butcher or not, from occupying or using said stall or any other part of said market, for the following reasons: First—When said person shall be guilty of any fighting, quarreling, abusive or indecent language in said market. Secondly—When said person shall neglect or refuse to obey the ordinances and regulations of said city relative to the cleanliness or order of said market, or shall more than once refuse or neglect to obey the lawful orders of said Clerk. Thirdly—When any person shall more than once offer or expose for sale, or sell any article prohibited by the ordinances of said city. Fourthly—When any person shall offer or expose for sale any article or thing used for food, the sale of which shall have been prohibited by the Common Council, or by the Board of Health of said city; and said Clerk shall immediately after such suspension report the same, with the reasons therefor, to the Common Council of said city, who may either make said suspension perpetual, or remit the same. And if any person so suspended shall offer for sale or sell any article in any of the markets of said city until permitted so to do by the Common Council, he shall be punished by a fine of not more than two hundred dollars, or by one year's imprisonment, or by both, in the discretion of the Court. It shall be the duty of said Clerk to notify every person so suspended by him of his or her suspension, in writing.

Powers of clerk to suspend persons having stalls for reasons specified.

Clerk to report reason of suspension to Council.

Penalty of persons so suspended for selling in market.

Clerk to notify persons suspended in writing.

SEC. 8. The Clerk of each market shall procure from the City Treasurer, and keep in a book, the names of all persons who have rented stalls in said markets. He shall let to all persons desiring the same, stands for the sale of vegetables, fish, fruits, game, poultry and garden stuff, charging them such rents therefor as the Common Council shall establish. He shall report to the Treasurer the names of all persons renting said stands; shall once in each month collect and pay into the treasury all rents due for said stands, and shall report and account under oath to the Controller for all moneys collected by him, stating in said account the names of all persons renting stands

Clerk to keep register.

Report names of persons renting.

To report to Controller monthly.

TITLE V. CHAPTER 34.

during the preceding month, the names of those who have paid their rents, and the amount paid by them; the names of those who have not paid, and the amount which they are in arrears; and that he has paid all sums collected by him up to the date of said report and account to the Treasurer; and he shall, at the same time, file with the Controller the Treasurer's receipt for said sums. And if any person renting any stand or stall be more than a month in arrears of his rent for the same, it shall be the duty of said Clerk to order said person to surrender his stand or to pay the rent so due within a week from the day of said order; and if said person does not comply with said order, then said Clerk shall remove him from said stand; any person resisting a Clerk of Market, or refusing or neglecting to obey his lawful orders under this section, shall be punished by a fine not to exceed one hundred dollars, or by imprisonment not to exceed six months.

Clerk to notify persons in arrears to surrender their stands.

Penalty for refusing to obey clerk.

Clerk to attend market during market hours.

SEC. 9. Each Clerk shall constantly attend the market under his charge during the time said markets are open for business.

Clerk to test weights and measures.

SEC. 10. In case of suspicion respecting the weight or quantity of any article sold, or offered for sale, by weight or measure, in any public market, it shall be the duty of the Clerk of said market to weigh or measure the same, and if he finds said article deficient, either in weight or quantity, he shall forthwith complain before the proper tribunal of the person selling or offering for sale said article, and said person shall, upon conviction thereof, be punished by a fine not to exceed one hundred dollars, or by not to exceed ninety days' imprisonment.

Clerk to examine weights and measures monthly.

Penalty for refusal to show weights &c.

SEC. 11. It shall be the duty of each Clerk of Markets, once in each month, or oftener, as he deems necessary, to inspect and examine all the weights, measures and beams used in weighing or measuring in his market. And if any person shall neglect or refuse to exhibit his or their weights, measures and beams, or any of them, for examination or inspection as aforesaid, or shall hinder, obstruct or molest said Clerk in the performance of this duty, said person shall be punished by a fine not to exceed one hundred dollars, or by imprisonment not to exceed ninety days.

Clerk to complain of persons using light weights.

SEC. 12. If, after such examination and inspection, said Clerk shall find that said weights, measures or beams, or either or any of them, are false and incorrect, and not according to the standard established by the laws of the State of Michigan, it shall be the duty of said Clerk to complain of the person using the said weights, measures or beams, and upon conviction thereof, said person shall be punished by a fine not exceeding fifty dollars, or by not exceeding thirty days' imprisonment, or both, in the discretion of the Court.

Clerk to exclude from market persons engaged in combination, forestalling, &c.

SEC. 13. It shall be the duty of each Clerk of Markets to exclude from his market all persons who shall be engaged in combinations to raise the price of provisions, or who shall have been convicted of forestalling; and any person thus excluded, who shall sell or offer for sale, any article in the market from which he or she has been so excluded, without the consent of said Clerk, shall be punished by a fine of five dollars, or by two days' imprisonment for each and every offence.

Signification of the word "stall."

Signification of the word "stand."

SEC. 14. The word stall, as used in this ordinance, and all ordinances relating to markets, shall signify the places inside of market buildings occupied by butchers for the sale of meat; the word "stand" shall signify all places in markets occupied by hucksters, pedlars, and sellers of vegetables, eggs, butter, poultry, game, garden stuff, fish, and all other articles permitted to be sold in markets, which are not to be sold from stalls, and shall comprise all tables, booths, fixtures, wagons, boxes, barrels, sleighs, carts, and vehicles of any kind, used for the purpose of exposure of goods for sale by said hucksters, pedlars and sellers.

CHAPTER XXXV.

Relative to the Sale and Inspection of Firewood.

Division of city for sale and inspection of wood.

SECTION 1. The city of Detroit shall be divided by the Woodward Avenue into two districts for the sale and inspection of firewood. All that portion of said city lying west of said avenue shall be called the Lower Wood Inspection District; and all that portion of said city lying east of said avenue, shall be called the Upper Wood Inspection District.

Number of wood Inspectors in each District.

SEC. 2. There shall be two Wood Inspectors appointed for each of said districts, one for the dock, the other for the wood market, and that in case of the inability of either of said Inspectors, through sickness or temporary absence from the city, to act, the other be empow-

TITLE V. CHAPTER 35.

ered to act in his place; and esch Wood Inspector, before entering upon the duties of his office, shall take and subscribe the same oaths, and file a bond in the sum of one thousand dollars, as is now required by law of other officers of the corporation.

Duties of

SEC. 3. It shall be the duty of said Wood Inspectors to be and remain at the public market for the sale of wood between the hours of seven o'clock in the morning and six o'clock in the evening, during each day, Sunday excepted; they shall station all vehicles containing wood brought to said market for sale, in a proper and suitable manner in said market, taking care especially that said vehicles do not in any manner obstruct the public streets of said city; they shall measure all loads or parcels of wood, offered or exposed for sale in or about said markets, for which they shall be paid a fee at the rate of six cents for each load or parcel drawn by a double team, and five cents for each load or parcel drawn by a single horse, measured by them, and upon payment to them of said fee, they shall give to the person owning said wood a certificate signed by them, stating that said wood has been measured by them, and how many cords or parts of cords it contains.

Rates of emoluments.

Seller to obtain certificate, &c.

SEC. 4. No person shall sell wood by the wagon load in said market, unless he shall first have obtained a certificate of one of the Inspectors of said city, and in addition to said certificate, said wood shall be stamped in various places by the Inspector, and if any person shall sell, or offer to sell, any wood by the load from any vehicle in said market, without said certificate and said stamp, he shall be punished by a fine not to exceed ten dollars, or by ten days' imprisonment.

Penalty.

Wood sellers not to stand on streets.

SEC. 5. No person shall stand in any street, alley or public ground of said city, save in or about the public markets designated by the Common Council, with any vehicle containing wood for sale; and every person exposing wood for sale in vehicles shall stand in such place and position in said public markets as the Inspectors shall direct; and any person violating the provisions of this section shall be punished by a fine not exceeding ten dollars, or by imprisonment not exceeding ten days.

Penalty.

Penalty for using false certificates.

SEC. 6. Any person who shall use a false certificate in the sale of firewood, or use a certificate given for one load of wood for another, shall, upon conviction thereof, be punished by fine not to exceed fifty dollars, or by imprisonment not to exceed forty days. TITLE V. CHAPTER 35.

SEC. 7. No person shall deliver wood sold from boats or other water craft in said city, unless said wood shall have been measured by one of the Inspectors of wood for said city, and the person selling such wood shall pay said Inspector his fees, at the rate of five cents per cord for each cord or portion of a cord so measured, and said Inspector shall have an office in some central situation near the river in his respective district, where notice may be left, when wood sold is ready for inspection, also publish the location of his office in the most public manner. And if any person shall deliver wood sold from boats or other water craft in said city, without the same shall have been in-inspected by one of the Inspectors of wood for said city, he shall be punished by a fine not to exceed ten dollars, or by imprisonment ten days.

Wood not to be delivered from boats till inspected.

Penalty.

SEC. 8. Inspectors of firewood shall be appointed at the same time and in the same manner as other officers are appointed, by the Common Council, and shall hold their offices for the term of one year, but the Wood Inspectors appointed on the second Tuesday of January, 1858, shall be the Inspectors for the present year.

Inspectors how appointed.

SEC. 9. Nothing in this ordinance shall be construed to affect or interfere with the sale of wood from private wood yards or places.

Not to affect sale from private yards

SEC. 10. This ordinance shall not take effect until five days after its passage, and the City Marshal shall, immediately after the passage of the same, post hand-bills at each of the public wood yards in said city, and other public places, notifying the public of the provisions of this ordinance relative to the sale of wood, and the time when the same shall go into effect.

When this ordinance to be in force.

TITLE VI.
CHAPTER 36.

TITLE SIX.

OF THE PREVENTION OF FIRES.

CHAPTER XXXVI.

Relative to the Fire Department of the City of Detroit.

Fire Department whom to consist of.

SECTION 1. That the Fire Department of said city shall consist of a Chief Engineer, two or more Assistant Engineers, and as many Fire Engine and Hook and Ladder Companies and Fire Wardens as the Common Council shall from time to time prescribe.

Chief and assistants by whom appointed.

Term of office

Chief to file bond.

SEC. 2. The Chief and Assistant Engineers shall be appointed by the firemen, from their own members, in the month of April of each year, with the consent and confirmation of the Common Council of said city, and shall, when so appointed, continue in office for a term of one year, or until their successors are duly appointed, confirmed and qualified. They shall take the oath of office prescribed by the charter, and the Chief Engineer shall file with the Clerk of the city a bond in the sum of two thousand dollars, conditioned for the faithful performance of his duty, which condition shall be in the language prescribed by the charter for the official bonds of city officers.

Number of assistants till ordered otherwise.

SEC. 3. Until the Common Council shall, by resolution or ordinance otherwise prescribe, there shall be two Assistant Engineers, to be designated as the First Assistant Engineer and the Second Assistant Engineer.

Number of members of each H. & L. and Engine Co.

Age of members.

To be recommended by Trustees.

Proviso.

SEC. 4. Each fire engine and hook and ladder company shall consist of not less than twenty nor more than sixty members, who shall be men of good moral character; shall have resided in the city at least three months, shall be over eighteen years of age, and shall be appointed members of companies by the Common Council upon recommendation of the Board of Trustees of the Fire Department, incorporated by an act entitled "An act to incorporate the Fire Department of the city of Detroit," approved February 14, 1840: *Provided, always*, That each fireman shall, within thirty days from the date of his appointment by the Common Council, become a member of the Fire Department, otherwise said appointment shall be null and void.

SEC. 5. The Fire Wardens and members of fire engine companies and hook and ladder companies, shall constitute and be the firemen of said city, and no person shall be eligible to the office of Chief or Assistant Engineer who is not a member of the Fire Department. Who to be firemen of the city; who to be eligible to the office of Chief or assistants

SEC. 6. Each fire engine and hook and ladder company shall appoint from their own members a foreman, a first assistant foreman and a second assistant foreman, and such other officers as they may by their own rules or by-laws prescribe. Company to appoint their officers.

SEC. 7. Each fire engine and hook and ladder company may, in the month of April of each year, nominate to the Common Council three of their members to be appointed Fire Wardens of said city for the ensuing year, and said Fire Wardens, together with the ex-officio Fire Wardens prescribed by the charter, shall be and constitute a Board of Wardens, who shall elect one of their number Chief Warden; and the Fire Wardens so appointed shall have all the duties and powers in the wards in which they reside, that have heretofore been imposed upon and granted to the "Fire Wardens appointed for the several wards:" *Provided,* That the Common Council may also appoint, on the nomination of the Chief Warden, three other Wardens for each ward, who shall, before their appointment, be members of the Fire Department, and whose special duty it shall be to attend to the prevention of fires in their respective wards. To nominate 3 members of company as Fire Ward'ns in April each year. Fire Ward'ns to appoint Chief Ward'n Proviso.

SEC. 8. The appointment of the Chief and Assistant Engineers shall be certified to the Common Council by the said Board of Trustees, or the proper officers thereof, and no person shall vote for or have any voice in the appointment of said Chief or Assistant Engineers, unless said person is a fireman and member of the Fire Department under the provisions of this ordinance. Appointment of chief and assistants to be certified to Council.

SEC. 9. The Chief and other engineers, upon an alarm of fire, shall immediately repair to the place where said fire is, and the Assistant Engineers shall report themselves to the Chief, or person having the command of the Department for the time being, and obey his orders. Any person willfully violating the provisions of this section shall be punished by a fine not to exceed one hundred dollars, or by imprisonment not to exceed three months. Chief to repair to fires when alarm given.

SEC. 10. The Chief Engineer shall have full power, control and command over all persons whatever at fires; he shall station the engines and apparatus of companies, and see to it that all persons do Chief to have full control at all fires.

TITLE VI. CHAPTER 36.

the duty prescribed by law and ordinance, and any person who shall disobey the lawful orders of said Chief Engineer, obstruct, hinder or resist him in the performance of the duties prescribed for him by this ordinance, shall be punished by a fine not to exceed one hundred dollars, or by imprisonment not to exceed three months.

Punishment for disobeying orders of chief.

To direct measures for extinguishing fires.

SEC. 11. That it shall be the duty of the Chief Engineer to direct at all fires all such measures as he may deem most advisable for the effectual extinguishment of the said fires, and also once in every month to examine the condition of the fire engines and other apparatus, together with the engine house belonging to the corporation, and report the same to the Common Council, at least once in six months, accompanied by the names and number of all the members of the Fire Department, and the respective companies to which they belong, which shall be annually published in the month of December, by the Clerk of said city, in such newspaper of the said city as shall be employed by the Common Council; and whenever any of the said fire engines or other fire apparatus shall require to be repaired, the Chief Engineer shall report the same to the Common Council, and he shall report in writing all accidents of fire that may happen in this city, with the causes thereof, as well as can be ascertained, and the number and description of the buildings destroyed or injured, together with the names of the owners or occupants, to the Clerk of the city, who shall keep a faithful register of the same.

To examine engines and apparatus once a month and report once in six months.

To report the repairs necessary to Council—buildings destroyed, names of owners, &c.

City Clerk to keep record of same.

Mayor and Council to enforce ordinance.

SEC. 12. It shall be the duty of the Mayor and members of the Common Council and of the Chief and other Engineers, to enforce the provisions of this ordinance.

Assistant to act in absence of Chief.

SEC. 13. In case of the absence or sickness of the Chief Engineer, the First Assistant shall act as Chief Engineer, and if the First Assistant shall be absent or sick, then the Second Assistant shall act as Chief, and in case neither the Chief or other Engineers are present at a fire, the Mayor shall designate some fireman to take his place.

Duties of Wardens relative to fires—relative to property.

SEC. 14. It shall be the duty of the Fire Wardens to be present at all fires, and under the command of the Chief Warden to act as a fire guard. And it shall be the duty of such fire guard to take charge and possession of all property removed from buildings at fires, and to deliver the same to the City Marshal, or in his absence, to a City Constable, to be delivered to the City Marshal to store, or otherwise protect the same until it is claimed by the owner or owners, and upon such claim to deliver up the same to the owner or owners, upon the payment to the City Marshal of all expenses necessarily and actually incurred in and about the care and protection of such property, and for which a receipt shall be given by the Chief Warden. And the said fire guard are hereby invested with all necessary authority for the purpose of taking charge and possession of such property, and at every fire every Warden shall report himself to the Chief Warden, and be subject to his directions, and the Chief Warden shall report himself to the Chief Engineer, and be subject to his direction, and to the direction of the other engineers of the Fire Department; and it shall be the further duty of said Fire Wardens to prevent the hose from being trodden on, and to keep all idle and suspected persons from the fire and its vicinity, and also to use all proper exertions within their power for the preservation of goods and other property endangered at fires; and all citizens are hereby enjoined and required to comply with the directions of any of said Fire Wardens: *Provided*, Such directions be not in opposition to the orders of the person having supreme control at said fire.

Wardens to report themselves to Chief Warden, and Chief Warden to report himself to Chief Engineer.

SEC. 15. There shall be assigned to each fire engine company and hook and ladder company, such engines, machines and apparatus as the Common Council may deem necessary for the extinguishment of fires, and it shall be the duty of each of said companies, as often as any fire shall break out within the district to which they are assigned, to repair immediately upon the alarm thereof to their respective engines, machines or apparatus, and convey them to or near the place where such fire shall happen, and then in conformity with the directions given them by the Chief Engineer or Engineer, shall work and manage the said engines, machines and apparatus, with implements and instruments thereto belonging, with all their skill and power; and when the fire is extinguished, shall not remove therefrom but by the direction of the Chief Engineer or of the other engineers, which direction being obtained, they shall return with their respective engines, machines and apparatus, together with the implements and instruments thereto belonging, to their several places of deposit, and as soon as may be thereafter, wash and clean the same, and for the more effectually keeping and preserving the fire engines from decay, the firemen, when the season of the year will permit, shall, by order of the Chief Engineer, draw out the fire engines, in order to wash, cleanse and ex-

Council to assign engines to the different companies.

Companies to remain at fires until otherwise ordered by Engineer.

ercise them, and if any fireman shall neglect said duty, and if he shall willfully neglect to attend to any fire as aforesaid, or leave his engine while at any fire, without permission, or not perform his duty on such occasion, without reasonable excuse, he shall on conviction, be punished by a fine not to exceed twenty-five dollars, or by imprisonment not to exceed thirty days.

Penalty for non-performance of duty at fires.

Firemen to procure certificates from Treasurer of Fire Department countersigned by City Clerk.

SEC. 16. Whenever any person shall be appointed a fireman under this ordinance, it shall be his duty to call on the Treasurer of the Fire Department and procure a certificate, within one month from the date of his election, countersigned by the City Clerk, specifying the name and number of the company to which he has been appointed; and if such certificate shall not be procured within that time the appointment shall be null and void.

Each company to report annually names of members

SEC. 17. It shall be the duty of each company organized under this ordinance, or which is now organized in said city, to report, once in each year, or oftener if required, the names and numbers of their members, to the said Board of Trustees.

When elections illegal.

Sec. 18. The election of any person as a member of a company which has the number of members authorized by this ordinance shall be void.

Chief and assistants to be elected by ballot.

SEC. 19. The Chief and Assistant Engineers shall be appointed by ballot of the firemen at the time and in the manner prescribed by the Constitution and By-Laws of the Fire Department.

No disturbance to be raised at the poles.

Penalty for disturbance.

SEC. 20. No person shall make any noise or disturbance, fight, quarrel or use any obscene, indecent, insulting or abusive language at the place and during the time the ballots are being received for Chief or Assistant Engineers. Any person violating the provisions of this ordinance shall be punished by a fine not to exceed one hundred dollars, or by imprisonment not to exceed six months, and in addition to said fine or imprisonment, may be sentenced to be dismissed or expelled as a fireman; and any person so dismissed or expelled, shall not again serve or act as a member of a company without the special permission of the Board of Trustees, and a re-appointment by the Council, as prescribed in this ordinance.

Chief to wear uniform hat on duty.

SEC. 21. The Chief Engineer shall wear a leather hat when on duty, with the words "Chief Engineer" painted legibly thereon, and shall carry a speaking trumpet.

SEC. 22. The First Assistant Engineer shall wear a leathern cap with the words "Engineer No. 1," painted on the frontispiece thereof; and the Second Assistant Engineer shall wear a leathern cap with the words "Engineer No. 2," painted on the frontispiece thereof; they shall also each carry a speaking trumpet. Assistants to wear caps.

SEC. 23. All persons who now are, or hereafter may be, employed by the city to ring fire alarms, shall immediately on the breaking out of a fire, ring the bells, and continue so to do during twenty minutes, unless the fire be sooner extinguished, under the penalty of not exceeding twenty dollars for every such omission: *Provided*, That when a chimney only shall be on fire either by day or by night said bells shall not be rung. Public bell ringers to ring twenty minutes. Proviso.

SEC. 24. It shall also be the duty of every watchman or patrol, upon the breaking out of any fire, to alarm the citizens by crying out "fire," and mentioning the street where it may be, on his going to and coming from the next and nearest watch stations, that the alarm may be rapidly passed from one watch station to another, and the firemen and citizens may thereby be generally directed where to repair. Watchmen to cry out "Fire" along their route.

SEC. 25. All persons who at a fire shall refuse to obey any order or direction given by a person duly authorized to order or direct, or who shall resist or impede any officer or other person in the discharge of his duty, shall, in the absence of sufficient excuse, be punished by fine not exceeding fifty dollars. The Chief Engineer, any Fire Warden, Assistant Engineer, Foreman or Assistant Foreman of a fire company, may arrest any such person and detain him in custody until the fire is extinguished, when the person making the arrest shall make to the City Attorney the proper complaint, under this section, against the person arrested. Persons refusing to obey orders of duly authorized officers to be fined—their arrest authorized.

SEC. 26. It shall be lawful for the Foreman or Assistant Foreman of any fire engine or other fire company, or for any member of the Common Council, Chief Engineer or Assistant, or any Fire Warden, to require the aid of any citizen or inhabitant in drawing an engine or other apparatus to the fire, or the aid of any bystander at a fire to work any engine or apparatus at the same, and on neglect or refusal to comply with such requisition, the offender shall be punished by a fine not to exceed twenty dollars, or by imprisonment not to exceed twenty days—unless some sufficient cause for such refusal and neglect is alleged at the time and made to appear upon the trial—and Foremen of companies and other officers may require the aid of citizens at fires. Penalty for neglect to comply.

TITLE VI. CHAPTER 36.

any such person may be arrested and proceeded with as is provided for persons arrested under section twenty-five of this ordinance.

Penalty for injuring public property.

SEC. 27. If any person shall willfully injure, in any manner, any hose, fire engine or other apparatus, or building containing the same, belonging to this city, the offender shall, for every such offence, forfeit and pay not to exceed the sum of one hundred dollars, or be imprisoned not to exceed three months, or both, in the discretion of the Court, besides being liable to an action for the recovery of the damages done.

Marshal and Constables to repair to fires and report to any member of Council.

SEC. 28. The Marshal and every Constable shall repair immediately on the alarm of fire, with his staff or badge of office, to the place where the fire may be, and report himself to any member of the Common Council, (who is hereby vested with full power in the premises,) for the preservation of the public peace, and the removal of all idle and suspected persons, or the preservation of property in the vicinity of the fire; and if the Marshal or any Constable shall neglect to comply with the provisions of this section, he shall pay a fine of not exceeding fifty dollars, and be subject to removal from office.

Penalty for neglect.

Hook, Ladder and Axe men when ordered by competent authority to cut down buildings, &c.

SEC. 29. The hook and ladder and axe men shall, under the direction of the Chief Engineer and two members of the Common Council present, or in the absence of the Chief Engineer, then under the direction of either of the Assistant Engineers and two members of the Common Council, or in the absence of all the Engineers, then under the direction of three members of the Common Council, cut down and remove any building, erection or fence, for the purpose of checking the progress of the fire.

Persons in charge of engines not to apply the same to private use.

SEC. 30. If any person having charge of any engine or other fire apparatus, shall suffer or permit the same to be applied to private uses without the consent of the Mayor, Chief Engineer or Common Council, he shall be punished by a fine not to exceed one hundred dollars, or by imprisonment not to exceed ninety days.

Hours at which engines may run on sidewalks.

SEC. 31. Any member of the Fire Department of the city of Detroit, or other person who is not a member of said Department, who shall hereafter run, place or wheel upon any sidewalk, or aid or assist in running or placing any fire engine, hook and ladder truck, or hose company cart, upon any sidewalk adjoining or laying alongside any paved street or alley in said city, between the hours of six o'clock A. M. and ten o'clock P. M., shall, for every such offence, on conviction thereof before the Recorder's Court of said city, be punished by a fine not exceeding five dollars with cost of prosecution; and if a member of the Fire Department by suspension or expulsion, or either, at the discretion of the Court.

False alarms how punished.

SEC. 32. It shall not be lawful for any person or persons, without reasonable cause, by outcry, or ringing the bells, or by proclaiming fire, or by any other means whatsoever, to make or circulate, or cause to be made or circulated in any ward in the city of Detroit, any false alarm of fire, and the person or persons so offending, shall be punished by a fine not exceeding one hundred dollars, or by imprisonment in the county jail not exceeding sixty days.

Age at which persons may be Firemen.

SEC. 33. No person under the age of eighteen years shall continue, or hereafter become a member of any fire engine, hose or hook and ladder company in said city, nor shall any fire engine company organize or permit any company or companies to take charge of their hose, or draw the same to and from fires, unless the members of said hose company or companies are duly qualified firemen under the laws of the State of Michigan and the ordinances of the City, and are members of the fire engine company whose hose shall be so taken in charge of or drawn. Any person under the age of eighteen years, who shall become a member of any fire engine, hose or hook and ladder company, shall be punished by a fine not to exceed ten dollars, or by imprisonment not to exceed five days for each and every occasion on which he shall parade, run to a fire or perform any other duty with said company, and the Chief Engineer of said city is hereby authorized to dismiss from any and every company connected with the Fire Department any person acting as fireman who is under eighteen years of age.

No person to sleep in engine houses. Exception.

SEC. 34. No person shall sleep or remain at night in any Fire Engine House, or in any Hook and Ladder House in said city, unless specially designated so to do by the Mayor, Common Council or Chief Engineer. No person shall play at cards, tipple, riot, or in any manner make any noise or disturbance in or about any such house. No person shall disturb any meeting of a fire company, or make any engine house or hook and ladder house a place of resort for indecent, lascivious, immoral or illegal purposes; any person violating the provisions of this section shall be punished by a fine not to exceed fifty dollars, or by imprisonment not to exceed ninety days.

Penalty for disturbing company meetings.

TITLE VI. CHAPTER 37.

Fire companies in force.

SEC. 35. The present companies organized and existing in said city are hereby continued in force. Fire engine companies numbered 1, 2, 3, 6, 7, 9 and 11, shall attend all fires in the second, third, fourth, sixth, seventh and tenth wards of said city, and engine companies numbered 4, 5, 8, 10 and 12, shall attend all fires occurring in the first, second, fifth, eighth and ninth wards of said city; but in cases of a general alarm all of said companies shall attend said fires, wherever they may occur in said city.

Districts.

Present Fire Wardens disbanded.

SEC. 36. The board or company of Fire Wardens now existing, are hereby disbanded, and chapter thirty-seven of the Revised Ordinanees of 1855, and all ordinances and parts of ordinances conflicting with this ordinance, are hereby repealed.

CHAPTER XXXVII.

Relative to the Prevention of Fires.

Of the board of Fire Wardens.

SECTION 1. The Fire Wardens shall constitute a board, a majority of whom, whether appointed or by virtue of their office, shall be a quorum for the purpose of considering the most efficient and prompt manner of discharging the duties imposed on them by the laws and ordinances of the city; they shall choose from their number a Chief and Secretary, at such time and in such manner as they may designate. The Fire Wardens of the respective wards shall notice and correct any infractions of the laws and ordinances made for the protection of the city from fires, in their respective wards particularly, and in the city generally, and shall make reports by their foreman, to be by them respectively chosen, of the state and police of their respective wards, as respects danger from exposure to fires, on the first Mondays of June and December in each year, to the Chief Warden, who shall make report of the same in reference to the city generally, to the Common Council; and the Board may impose such fines upon the members as, in their judgment, may best secure the performance of the duties of said Fire Wardens, both at fires and in visiting buildings, and in other duties in their several wards, and for non-attendance at regular or special meetings of the Wardens; and any disobedience to such rules shall be reported to the Common Council, and shall subject the Fire Warden so disobeying to fine and removal by the Common Council.

Semi-annual inspection of the city.

SEC. 2. It shall be the duty of the Fire Wardens, or either of them, in their respective wards, twice in each year, viz.: in the months of May and November, and as much oftener as may be deemed proper, between sunrise and sunset, to enter into any house or building, lots, yards or premises in said city, and examine the fire places, hearths, chimneys, stoves and pipes thereto, ovens, boilers or other apparatus likely to cause fire; also, the places where ashes may be deposited, and all places where any gunpowder, hemp, flax, tow, hay, straw, rushes, shavings or other combustible materials may be lodged; and the said Fire Wardens shall give such directions in regard to the several foregoing matters as they or any of them may think expedient, either as to the removal and alteration, or better care and management thereof; which directions shall be obeyed and complied with by the person or persons directed in that behalf, and at their expense.

Of cleaning chimneys.

SEC. 3. The said Fire Wardens shall also have authority to cause chimneys to be burned out or otherwise cleaned, whenever they shall deem it necessary, and to require the tenant or tenants, owner or owners of any blacksmith's shop so to alter or construct (as the case may require) the chimneys in said shop as to prevent sparks of fire from passing into the open air, and may require the ceiling or sides of any shop or any part thereof to be plastered. Every occupant of premises whose chimneys shall take fire, except when burned out under the direction or by the permission of a Fire Warden, shall be be fined one dollar for each infraction of the law; and also to remove or abate, with the consent of the Mayor or any Alderman, (and in neglect or refusal of the owner or occupant,) any cause from which immediate danger of fire may be apprehended, at the expense of the person who should have done the same; and to remove or abate, in manner above prescribed, any other cause whatever from which immediate danger of fire may be apprehended, at the expense of the person or persons occasioning the same. The said Fire Wardens are hereby empowered at any regular or special meeting of their Board, to require that chimneys shall be swept or cleaned by owners or occupants, as the case may be, at such periods, and under such regulations as they may prescribe; and for every case of neglect or refusal, the parties offending shall forfeit and pay a penalty of one dollar,

Penalty if they take fire.

Abating cause of danger in chimneys.

and for every subsequent case of neglect or refusal, after being thereto specially required by a Fire Warden, a penalty of one dollar in addition.

Penalty for disobeying Fire Warden.

SEC. 4. If any person or persons shall neglect or refuse so to comply with any such directions as any of said Fire Wardens may give in the premises, or shall obstruct or hinder any Fire Warden or his assistants in the performance of his duty, the person so offending shall forfeit and pay for every such neglect, non-compliance or hindrance, a sum not exceeding fifty dollars, and for every day which shall elapse after the time allotted for such removal, alteration, better care or management, without compliance with such directions, the said person shall also forfeit and pay a further and additional sum of five dollars; and all expenses caused in carrying into effect the directions of the Fire Wardens, shall in the first instance be paid by the occupant of the premises, and shall be deducted from the rent payable by him, her or them, unless such directions were rendered necessary by the act or default of said occupant, or there be a special agreement to the contrary between the landlord and said occupant; and it shall also be the duty of said Fire Wardens to ascertain whether or not their directions are duly complied with, and in case of non-compliance, or in case of any violation of this chapter, to report the names of all the offenders, with the particular circumstances, to the Common Council, who may thereupon cause such offenders to be prosecuted for the recovery of the penalties incurred by them.

Owners of premises liable for expenses of executing direction of Wardens.

Securing stove pipe and burning chimneys.

SEC. 5. No pipe of any stove or franklin shall be put up in any house or building, unless it be conducted into a chimney made of brick or stone; nor shall any person at any time set fire to any chimney for the purpose of cleaning the same, without previous consent of the Fire Warden of the proper ward; any person putting up, or procuring to be put up, the pipe of any stove or franklin, or doing any other act contrary to this section, shall for every offence forfeit five dollars, and the further sum of one dollar for every twenty-four hours the same shall remain so put up, after notice by any Fire Warden to alter the same.

How chimneys shall be constructed.

SEC. 6. Every chimney hereafter to be erected, and all chimneys whatever, shall be plastered with lime and sand on the inside thereof, under a penalty of twenty-five dollars, and a further penalty of ten dollars for every fifteen days' neglect to alter or take down the same, after a notice given by any Fire Warden for that purpose. It shall be the duty of the Engineers or Fire Wardens to take notice of all chimneys when the same are being constructed, and ascertain whether they are in conformity with the requirements of this chapter, and if not, make report to the Common Council. Chimneys shall be so constructed or altered as to admit of the flues therein being swept or cleaned from top to bottom, under the same penalties for neglect or refusal as are prescribed in section three.

Of carrying fire through streets.

SEC. 7. No person shall carry fire in or through any street or lot except the same be placed or carried in some close and secure pan or vessel, under a penalty of five dollars for each offence.

Securing ashes.

SEC. 8. No ashes, except at manufactories where ashes are used, shall be kept or deposited in any part of this city, unless the same be in a close and secure metalic or earthen vessel, or brick or stone ash-room, under the penalty of one dollar for every twenty-four hours the same shall remain after notice from a Fire Warden to remove the same.

Of fire works and fire arms

SEC. 9. No person shall fire or set off any squib, cracker, gunpowder or fireworks, or fire any gun or pistol in any part of this city, unless by written permission of the Mayor or two Aldermen, which permission shall limit the time of such firing, and shall be subject to be revoked at any time by the Common Council; and any person or persons violating any of the provisions of this section, shall forfeit the penalty of five dollars for each and every offence.

Of cannon.

SEC. 10. Every person firing a cannon within this city, unless by permission of the Mayor or two Aldermen, shall forfeit the penalty of twenty-five dollars: *Provided*, That nothing in this or the preceding section shall be construed to prohibit any military company from firing any gun or cannon when authorized by their commanding officer or officers.

Of scuttles.

SEC. 11. Every dwelling house or other building more than one story in height within this city, shall have a scuttle through the roof, and a convenient and suitable stairway or ladder leading to the same; and any person constructing such dwelling house or building, without such scuttle, and every owner of any such house or building now erected, (not having other permanent and convenient means of access to the roof,) neglecting to comply with the requisitions of this section for the space of thirty days after notice from a Fire Warden, shall forfeit

TITLE VI. CHAPTER 37.

twenty-five dollars, and the further sum of five dollars for every ten days the non-compliance shall continue to exist.

Of shavings and combustibles.

SEC. 12. It shall not be lawful for any person or persons to have in his or her possession, any shavings, wood or fuel of any description, combustibles, or any materials that may occasion hazard or danger of fire, unless the same shall be placed in such situation, and be secured in such manner as shall be directed by the Fire Wardens, or either of them, of the ward in which either of the before enumerated articles shall be deposited; and all carpenters, cabinet makers, turners, coach makers, wheelwrights, coopers and others using any trade by which shavings are made, shall respectively, at the close of each day, on leaving off work, cause the place where such shavings are, to be swept, and the shavings to be carefully gathered and placed in boxes, or to be otherwise compactly and securely stowed in some safe place, remote from danger, by means of fire or candle light, and so to be kept until the same shall be taken away from such premises as aforesaid, under the penalty of five dollars for each omission or offence therein.

Fires in the streets.

SEC. 13. It shall not be lawful to burn any shavings in any street, road or lane, or to kindle any fire or any other combustible matter in any street, road or lane, or on any wharf in this city, under a penalty not exceeding ten dollars for each offence, to be recovered from any person or persons aiding or assisting therein.

Keeping of hay and straw.

SEC. 14. No person shall have, put or keep any hay or straw uncovered, in stack or pile, within three hundred yards of any building within the limits of this city: *Provided, however*, That nothing herein shall be construed to prevent landing hay or straw on any of the wharves of this city, or to prevent carting the same to or from any part of the saaid city; nor shall any person have, put or keep, within the said city, any hay or straw, hemp, flax, tow, shavings or rushes, in any stable or other building which is, or shall be, within such distance from any chimney, hearth or fire place, or place for depositing ashes, nor in any dwelling house whatever, as may be deemed unsafe or dangerous by the Fire Warden of the proper ward, under a penalty not exceeding twenty-five dollars for each and every offence, to be recovered with costs of suit, and the further sum of ten dollars for every twenty-four hours the same shall so remain after due notice given in writing to the offender, by the Fire Warden or other officer. TITLE VI. CHAPTER 37.

SEC. 15. No powder shall be deposited in any magazine, unless the same be approved by the Common Council. Powder.

SEC. 16. The Common Council shall appoint a suitable person to be the keeper of the magazine, and he shall be entitled to demand and have twenty-five cents on each keg of powder received, stored and delivered by him, to be paid by the person for whom it is stored. Keeper of magazine.

SEC. 17. If any fireman, during a fire, and in the vicinity thereof, shall discover in any building a greater quantity than twenty-eight pounds of powder, it shall be lawful for him to seize, without warrant from any magistrate, and convert the same as forfeited to the use of the Fire Department. Powder to be seized.

SEC. 18. There shall not be kept within the limits of this city, (except in the magazine of powder of the United States, or of this State,) at any one time, in any one house and its appurtenances, or in any one store and its appurtenances, any greater quantity of gunpowder than the weight of twenty-eight pounds; which twenty-eight pounds of gunpowder shall be well secured in metal canisters, with metal stoppers or covers, neither of which shall contain more than seven pounds weight. All gunpowder which shall be kept in this city, contrary to the meaning and provisions of this chapter, shall be forfeited by the person or persons so keeping the same; and it shall be lawful for the Mayor, Engineer or any Fire Warden to seize the same in manner as provided in section seventeen, and the person or persons so offending shall also forfeit the sum of one hundred dollars for every hundred weight of gunpowder, and in that proportion for a greater or less quantity, so kept contrary to the true intent and meaning of this chapter, to be recovered with costs of suit in the Recorder's Court of this city. Where and how powder to be kept.

SEC. 19. It shall be the duty of the Chief Warden or City Marshal to dispose of all gunpowder forfeited and seized as provided in the preceding section, and pay the proceeds arising therefrom to the Treasurer of the Fire Department, for the use of said Department, taking his receipt therefor, and report the same to the President of said Department. And to avoid dangers from gunpowder laden on board of any vessel arriving at this port, *Be it further ordained*, Chief Warden or Marshal to dispose of powder seized, &c.

TITLE VI. CHAPTER 37.

Commanders and owners of vessels having powder on board, how to land the same.

That the commander or owners of every vessel arriving at this port, and having gunpowder on board, shall, wtthin twenty-four hours after her arrival before this city, and before such vessel shall be hauled alongside of any wharf, pier or quay, within the said city, land the said gunpowder by means of a boat or boats, or other small craft, at any place out of the limits, viz.: above or below this city, on the Detroit river, and shall cause the same to be stored in some safe place beyond the said limits, until the same shall be conveyed to such magazine as shall be provided by the corporation for the storing of gunpowder, on pain of forfeiting all such gunpowder.

Of conveying powder through the streets.

SEC. 20. For the more safe conveyance of gunpowder through the city, to or from any magazine or powder house, the store keeper shall procure and provide good canvas, tow cloth or leathern bags, or cases, in order to cover all casks of gunpowder that may be conveyed as aforesaid; and no cartmen or other person shall cart or carry through any avenue, street or lane of this city, by means of any cart, carriage, or by hand or otherwise, any gunpowder, except in tight casks, well headed and hooped, which casks shall be put into such canvas, tow cloth or leathern bags or cases as aforesaid, in such manner as entirely to cover such cask therewith, and the mouths of such bags or cases shall be securely tied, so that no gunpowder may be spilled or scattered in the passage thereof, on pain of forfeiting all such gunpowder as shall be conveyed through any of the avenues, streets or lanes aforesaid, in any other manner than is hereby directed.

Of lading or unlading powder in the city.

SEC. 21. No person, excepting as aforesaid, shall be permitted to lade or unlade any greater quantity of gunpowder than twenty-eight pounds, in or from any vessel at any of the slips or wharves in the city, under the penalty of forfeiting a sum not exceeding one hundred dollars for each offence.

Lights in stables.

SEC. 22. No owner or occupant of any livery or other stable within this city, nor any person in the employment of such owner or occupant, shall use therein any lighted candle or other light, except the same be securely kept within a horn, tin or glass lantern, under a penalty not exceeding ten dollars for each offence, to be recovered with costs of suit.

Liability of parents and masters.

SEC. 23. If any offence shall be committed against this chapter by any child, apprentice or servant, the forfeiture and penalty shall be recovered from and paid by the parent, master or mistress of the party offending.

CHAPTER XXXVIII.

Relative to the Erection of certain Buildings within certain limits.

Wooden buildings where prohibited.

SECTION 1. No person shall hereafter erect or place any building or any part of a building within the following limits, unless such building or part of a building shall be constructed of stone or brick, with party or fire walls of the same material, rising at least ten inches above the roof, if the same be covered with metal or slate; if with wood, then at least two feet, viz.: Beginning at the channel bank, foot of Dequindre street, thence northerly to a point within one hundred feet of the south line of Jefferson avenue, thence easterly parallel with Jefferson avenue, and one hundred feet distant therefrom to the east line of the city limits; thence northerly, to a point one hundred feet north of the north line of Jefferson avenue; thence westerly, parallel with said avenue and one hundred feet distant therefrom, to the centre of Dequindre street; thence northerly to the centre of the block between Congress and Fort streets; thence westerly to the centre of Rivard street; thence northerly to the centre of the block between Lafayette and Croghan streets; thence westerly to the centre of St. Antoine street; thence northerly to within one hundred feet of the southerly line of Gratiot street; thence northeasterly, parallel with said Gratiot street, to the centre of Russell street; thence northerly to a point within one hundred feet north of the north line of Gratiot street; thence southwesterly, parallel within one hundred feet of said Gratiot street to the centre of Beaubien street; thence northerly along said street to the alley between Elizabeth and Columbia streets; thence westerly along said alley to the west line of the Lambert Beaubien farm; thence northerly along said westerly line of said Lambert Beaubien farm to the north line of Wilkins street; thence westerly to the alley between Woodward avenue and Park street; thence southerly, parallel with said Woodward avenue, to the alley between Columbia and Elizabeth streets; thence westerly to the Grand River Road along said alley; thence southeasterly to the centre of First street; thence southerly along said street to within

TITLE VI. CHAPTER 38.

one hundred feet of the north line of Michigan avenue; thence westerly, parallel with said Michigan avenue to the west line of the Woodbridge farm; thence southerly to a point one hundred feet south of the south line of Michigan avenue, thence easterly, parallel with said avenue, to the west line of the Jones farm; thence southerly along said west line to the alley between Howard and Abbott streets; thence westerly along said alley to Thompson street; thence southerly along said Thompson street, due south, to the channel of the river; thence easterly along the channel bank of Detroit river to the place of beginning. And if any building not made and constructed of stone, or brick, or other incombustible material, shall be erected or placed within the aforesaid prescribed limits, contrary to the provisions of this section, the owner or owners, builder or builders thereof, shall severally forfeit a penalty of fifty dollars for each and every offence, and also a penalty of fifty dollsrs for each and every week such building shall remain within said limits as above prescribed.

Penalty.

Barns and wood houses of certain size permitted.

SEC. 2. Nothing contained in the preceding section shall prohibit the erection within the aforesaid prescribed limits, of any building of wood which shall not be more than eight feet square, nor of any wood house for keeping and storing of fire wood, which shall not exceed twenty feet in length, twelve feet in width, and twelve feet in height, nor of any barn which shall not exceed twenty-four feet in length, sixteen feet in width, and not more than twelve feet in height from the common surface of the earth to the top of the plates, with a roof not to exceed one-quarter pitch, provided such small buildings or wood house or barn shall not be made to front upon any street: *Provided*, That nothing in this section contained shall be construed to allow more than one such barn or wood-shed on any one lot or premises used as one tenement.

Partition walls.

SEC. 3. The limits prescribed in section one of this chapter, shall be known as the fire limits of the city of Detroit, and the whole of the ground included within said prescribed limits shall be deemed and taken to be within said fire limits; and in all buildings hereafter to be erected of stone or brick, in blocks of two or more buildings, within said limits, there shall be erected partition walls running at right angles with the street upon which such building shall front, or as nearly at right angles with said street, as the plan of the city will admit of, constructed of stone or brick, at least one foot in thickness, and extending at least ten inches above the roof, if such roof be covered with metal or slate; but if of wood, then at least two feet above the roof of such building; and every person, whether owner, part owner or builder, who shall erect or cause to be erected a building or part of a building contrary to the provisions of this section, shall forfeit the penalty of fifty dollars for every month during which such building shall remain so erected.

Certain repairs prohibited.

SEC. 4. No person shall repair any wooden building partially destroyed by fire, nor raise or elevate from the ground any wooden building now standing within said limits, by constructing thereunder or thereon another story or part of a story, or in any other way increase the height of said building, unless he shall have previously obtained permission from the Common Council to do so, and in no case where the proposed repairs or alterations will increase the fire risks, shall such permission be granted; and if any person shall violate the provisions of this section, then he shall forfeit a penalty of fifty dollars, and also a penalty of fifty dollars for each and every week said building shall remain so raised or erected.

Penalty.

Building not to be removed within the fire limits.

SEC. 5. No person shall remove any building of wood from one part, or section, or lot within such fire limits, to any other part, section or lot within the same: *Provided*, That it shall be competent for the Common Council, on special application, in their discretion, to grant leave to the owner or occupant of any lot or premises to remove any such building from one part of said lot or premises to another part of the same lot or premises. And in case any person shall violate the provisions of this section, he shall forfeit the like penalty of fifty dollars; and also a further penalty of fifty dollars for each and every week such building shall be permitted to remain upon the place to which it shall have been removed.

Penalty.

Height of building without fire limits.

SEC. 6. No person shall build, erect or place any building or part of a building, more than twenty-six feet in height, measuring from the established grade, or common surface of the ground of the street or alley upon which such building shall front, to the top of the plate of such building; nor shall the roof thereof exceed a quarter pitch, unless such building shall be constructed of stone or brick, as provided in section one of this chapter, in any part of the city whatever. And any owner or owners, builder or builders, for hire, who shall at any

TITLE VI. CHAPTER 38.

time build or place any such building within the limits of the city, contrary to the provisions of this section, shall each and severally, upon conviction thereof before the Recorder's Court, pay a fine for each and every offence not exceeding fifty dollars; and the owners thereof shall, on conviction, be subject to a like penalty of fifty dollars for each and every week he, she or they shall suffer such building (to be hereafter erected,) to remain within the limits of the city: *Provided*, That nothing in this chapter shall prohibit the erection of steeples or cupola upon any church or any public building, or manufactory establishment.

Lime kilns prohibited.

SEC. 7. No person shall erect or cause to be erected within the limits of the city, any lime kiln or building to be used in the manufacture or burning of lime; and if any person shall violate the provisions of this section, he shall forfeit a penalty of one hundred dollars, and also a penalty of one hundred dollars for each and every week such lime kiln or building shall be used for the manufacture or burning of lime.

Ordinance suspended in certain cases till June 1st, 1859.

SEC. 8. The operation of the provisions of the aforesaid ordinance, to which this is amendatory, shall be and are hereby suspended, so far as relates to any territory added to or embraced within the fire limits since the first day of March, 185E, until the first day of June, 1859, from and after which time the said ordinance and all its provisions shall be in force and of effect as if this ordinance had not been passed.

TITLE SEVEN.

OF THE PUBLIC HEALTH.

CHAPTER XXXIX.

Relative to Small Pox.

SECTION 1. That the keepers of all taverns, hotels and boarding houses within the limits of this city, shall be, and they are hereby required, whenever the small pox shall be found to exist therein, to close them immediately, and to keep them closed against all customers and lodgers until the patients are removed, and such tavern, hotel or boarding house shall be thoroughly cleansed and ventilated, under a penalty not exceeding one hundred dollars for each case of the small pox within their premises, to be recovered in the Recorder's Court, with costs.

Taverns and boarding houses where small pox is to close doors

SEC. 2. That every keeper of a tavern, hotel, boarding house or house within the limits aforesaid, within whose premises any person or persons may at any time be sick of small pox, shall be, and he or she is hereby required to exhibit openly and publicly at his or her front door or gate, a sign, with the words "small pox," distinctly and legibly written or printed thereon, under such penalty for every willful omission, not exceeding fifty dollars with costs, as the Recorder's Court may on complaint impose.

Signs to be placed on houses where small pox exists.

SEC. 3. That it is hereby made the duty of every practising physician within the limits of the said city, to report in writing to the Clerk of the city, or to any member of the Common Council, every case of the small pox which he may be called to visit or examine; which report shall contain, as near as may be, a description of the location in the city of each case, and the name of the patient, under a penalty not exceeding one hundred dollars for each day such report shall be withheld.

Physicians to report cases of small pox.

SEC. 4. That it shall not be lawful for any person or persons who may have been, or may be diseased as aforesaid, to go at large within the limits aforesaid, until advised by a physician that said going at large will not endanger the health of others.

Diseased persons not to go at large.

SEC. 5. If any person so diseased shall be found going at large, it shall be competent for the Mayor, Recorder, or either of the Alder-

Mayor may confine persons having.

men, to send him forthwith to some suitable place to be provided, and if need be, to confine him there so long as the public safety may require.

CHAPTER XL.

Relative to Grave Yards.

Public grave yards.

SECTION 1. That the grave yards lying north of the Fort Gratiot turnpike, are hereby declared to be the only public grave yards within the limits of the city of Detroit, and the plan thereof respecting lots for interment, is hereby continued; and all graves shall be at least five feet deep.

Duty of Sexton.

SEC. 2. It shall be the duty of the Sexton to superintend the grave yards, to take charge of the city hearse, and when required by the friends of any deceased person, or by the Director of the Poor of the said city, he shall, within a reasonable time, cause to be dug a grave of suitable dimensions, agreeably to the preceding section, and shall bury the corpse therein; and when it shall be required of the Sexton, he shall deliver the coffin at the house where the corpse may be, furnish a horse for the hearse, and convey the corpse to the grave.

Where corpses to be buried.

SEC. 3. It shall not be lawful for any person or persons to inter or cause to be interred, the corpse of any deceased person in any part of said city, excepting in the public grave yards aforesaid.

The Sexton may demand and receive fees.

SEC. 4. The Sexton may demand and receive for his services the following fees, to wit: for digging a grave and burying the corpse, one dollar and fifty cents; for delivering the coffin at the house where the corpse may be, twenty-five cents; for furnishing a horse and carrying the corpse to the grave, one dollar and seventy-five cents: *Provided,* That whenever the corpse is to be buried less than one mile beyond the limits of said city, the Sexton shall be entitled to demand and receive for digging a grave and burying the corpse, two dollars, and for furnishing a horse and carrying the corpse to the grave, one dollar and seventy-five cents.

Lots and half lots how purchased.

SEC. 5. Any person who may be desirous of purchasing a lot in the new cemetery, may make application to the City Clerk, and if the same be granted, the applicant shall pay the sum of ten dollars to the City Treasurer, and take his certificate therefor. Nothing in this section shall prohibit the sale of half lots, if any there should be, at the price of five dollars, and no lot shall be divided for this purpose, so long as any half lot remains unsold.

Clerk to convey lots, &c.

SEC. 6. The purchaser or his assigns shall deposit said duplicate with the City Clerk, who shall thereupon execute and deliver a deed for the lot described therein, to the person entitled thereto, and charge the Treasurer for the price paid.

No one to be buried without permission.

SEC. 7. No person shall inter, or cause to be interred, the corpse of any deceased person in either of said grave yards without the permission of the person or persons, or corporation owning the lot.

Penalties.

SEC. 8. Any person or persons who shall violate any of the provisions of this chapter, shall forfeit and pay a sum not exceeding twenty-five dollars with costs of suit; and if any Sexton shall neglect or refuse to perform the duties herein required, or demand for his services a sum greater than is provided by the fourth section of this chapter, he shall, on conviction thereof before the Recorder's Court, be fined in a sum not exceeding twenty-five dollars with costs of suit.

Clerk to register lots sold

SEC. 9. The Clerk shall keep a register of all lots heretofore or hereafter to be sold in the new cemetery, by which it shall appear the name of the person or persons owning the lot, the description of the same, the price paid therefor, and the time when the deed was executed and delivered.

Alleys in grave yards not to be obstructed.

SEC. 10. It shall not be lawful for any person to obstruct or cause to be obstructed, nor permit or suffer any obstruction occasioned by him or those under whom he claims, to be or remain in any of the alleys of the public grave yards of said city. And it shall be the duty of the Sexton to remove all such obstructions at the expense of the persons occasioning or permitting the same as aforesaid, which upon conviction, shall be included in the fine adjudged against him.

Lots for burying strangers.

SEC. 11. The Common Council shall, whenever necessary, designate suitable lots in the new cemetery for the interment of the corpse of any deceased poor person or stranger; and it shall be the duty of the Sexton to inter any such corpse in any lot so designated, when he shall be of opinion that such corpse cannot be lawfully interred in any other place in the public grave yards.

SEC. 12. It shall be the duty of the Sexton to keep a register of all interments made in the public grave yards, in which shall be stated

TITLE VII. CHAPTER 41.

A Register to be kept of interments and report to be made to the Common Council.

the name of the deceased person, the time of his decease, his late rasidence, the place of his birth, his occupation, and the disease or complaint of which he died, and to report the same on Mondays of each week to the City Clerk; such report to include the particulars of all interments for the full week ending on Saturdays previous to the date of such report; the Sexton shall also at the expiration of his term of office, deliver said register to his successor in office; and no person or persons other than the Sexton or his employees, shall dig or open any grave in the said grave yards, on pain of fine not to exceed fifty dollars for each offence, on conviction therefor.

CHAPTER XLI.

Relative to Sluices and Low Grounds.

Assessment for low grounds, sluices, &c.

SECTION 1. Whenever it may be deemed necessary or expedient to make and open any sluice, ond make any wharf or embankmedt on the margin of the Detroit river, or fill up any low grounds or lots covered or partially covered with water, adjacent to said river, or when it shall be necessary for the abatement of any nuisance to fill up or level any lots or low grounds not adjacent to said river, but within the limits of said city, the Common Council shall, by a written resolution to be entered on their journal, authorize some competent person to make an assessment for making such sluice, wharf, embankment, or filling up such low grounds or abating such nuisances; and upon approving and filing such assessment, the Common Council shall order that the owner, occupant or proprietor of such wharf, low grounds or lots, (describing them,) shall make such sluice, wharf or embankment, or fill up such low grounds or lots, or abate such nuisance, within a certain time, and in such manner as may be in such order specified.

Marshal to give notice of order to fill low grounds.

SEC. 2. It shall be the duty of the Marshal to give notice in writing to such owner, occupant or proprietor personally, or by leaving the same at his place of residence in said city, requiring him to comply with such order, a copy of which shall be annexed to such notice, and also that within ten days after the service of such notice, he shall enter into a bond to the city of Detroit, with approved security, conditioned for the performance and execution of such order, and the Marshal shall make due return or report to the Common Council of his doings in the premises: *Provided*, That if any such person cannot be found, or has no place of residence in said city, the Marshal shall cause such notice to be published four weeks in some paper in said city, unless the Common Council shall otherwise order, and an affidavit thereof shall be filed with the Clerk.

When Council may order a lot to be filled.

SEC. 3. Whenever it shall appear to the Common Council that the notice required by the preceding section has been given, and that such bond has not been executed, within the time limited therefor, then the Common Council may cause such sluice, wharf or embankment to be finished and completed, or such low ground or lots to be filled up, or such nuisance abated in such manner as they may deem expedient and necessary; and the expense thereof shall be deemed a valid assessment, from the time of filing the same as aforesaid.

Clerk to deliver the assessment to collector to be collected.

SEC. 4. The Clerk shall record in the assessment register all assessments made by virtue of this chapter, and the date of the same; and immediately after said work mentioned in said order shall have been finished and completed, the Clerk shall make out and deliver to the Collector a copy of such assessment, to be collected as other special assessments.

CHAPTER XLIII.

To prescribe and regulate the manner of drawing Jurors in the matter of Draining Wet and Low Lands.

Common Council may declare whose lands they deem should be drained.

SECTION 1. Whenever the said Common Council shall deem it necessary to drain any swamp, marsh, wet or low lands, in accordance with the power conferred upon said Council by subdivision twenty-fifth of section twenty-second, of chapter fifth, of the Revised Charter of said city, they shall so declare by resolution, which resolution shall describe the size and location of the ditch proposed to be opened for draining said lands, and shall also describe what private lands, if any, it will be necessary to take to make said ditch. A copy of said resolution, certified to by the City Clerk, shall be delivered by said Clerk to the City Attorney, who shall file the same in the Recorder's Court, and move said Court for the drawing of a jury to determine

Certified copy to be given to City Attorney by clerk.

TITLE VII. CHAPTER 42.

the necessity or propriety of opening said ditch, and whether the benefits which will accrue to the owner or owners of any lands from the opening of said ditch, will or will not be equal to any damages he or they will sustain thereby.

Recorder's court to order City Marshal, or other officer, to write the names of Jurors.

SEC. 2. Said Court, upon being satisfied that the proper resolution has been filed by said Attorney, shall order the City Marshal, his assistant or other officer of said city in attendance upon said Court, to write down the names of twelve freeholders of Wayne county, who shall be approved by the Court as qualified to serve upon said jury.

Court to issue summons for Jurors.

SEC. 3. Said Court shall issue a summons to the Marshal, his assistant or other officer of said city having authority to serve process in said Court, commanding him to summons said twelve freeholders to be and appear in said Court, on some day to be named in said writ, which shall not be less than seven days after the issuance thereof, and said summons shall be served at least three days before the return day, thereof, and be returned in the same manner as a summons for petit jurors in said Court, and the persons thus summoned shall be bound to attend said Court and serve until discharged, and said Court shall impose upon them a fine of not more than five dollars for each day's non-attendance or neglect to serve in said Court, but they shall be exempted and excused by the Court for the same reasons that petit jurors may be exempted and excused.

Penalty for non-attendance of Jurors.

City Attorn'y to publish notice of the ordering of Jury.

SEC. 4. The City Attorney shall cause to be published in the daily newspaper printed by the contractor to print for the city, and in one other daily newspaper of said city, a notice to all whom it may concern that said jury has been ordered, the purpose for which and the time when and the place where they will be impanneled, which notice shall be published at least four consecutive days before said return day, and proof of publication thereof shall be filed in said Court on return day.

Persons interested may challenge Jurors.

SEC. 5. Any person who shall appear upon said return day and file an affidavit in said Court that he or she has an interest in any private land proposed to be taken, and showing to the satisfaction of said Court that he or she has such interest, shall be allowed to challenge any person summoned to appear upon said jury for cause, in the same manner as is allowed in civil actions under the laws of the State.

SEC. 6. Said Court shall have power to order talesmen to be summoned to fill said jury. Court may order talesmen.

SEC. 7. Said jury, when filled, shall be sworn to discharge their duties faithfully, and shall be advised by the City Attorney concerning their duties whenever they request it; they shall go upon the line of said ditch and examine the land proposed to be taken. Jurors to be sworn and advised by City Attorn'y

SEC. 8. They shall report to said Court in writing, which shall be signed by them, and said Court shall appoint a day upon which said report shall be received and filed. Jurors to report to court in writing.

SEC. 9. A copy of the report of said jury, certified to by the Clerk of said Court, shall be recorded by the City Clerk, in the book of street opening records, and also in the records of said Court. Report to be recorded by City Clerk.

SEC. 10. This ordinance shall take effect and be in force from and after five days after the passage thereof.

CHAPTER XLIII.

To provide for the Opening and Cleaning of Sewer Pools.

SECTION 1. That it shall be and hereby is made the duty of Overseers of Highways to clean and keep open and unobstructed the grates or other openings of pools within their respective wards, connecting with any of the public sewers of said city, so that at all times said grates or other openings shall be unobstructed and in condition to perform the office of carrying off the water from the public streets of said city.

SEC. 2. This ordinance shall take effect and be in force from and after its passage.

TITLE VIII.
CHAPTER 44.

TITLE EIGHT.

OF THE PUBLIC PEACE.

CHAPTER XLIV.

Relative to Breaches of the Peace and Disorderly Conduct.

Persons concealed for the purpose of crime.

SECTION 1. Any person who may hereafter be found lurking, lying in wait, or concealed in any house or other building, or in any yard or premises within the limits of said city, with intent to do any mischief, or to pilfer, or commit any crime or misdemeanor whatever, shall, for every such offence, on conviction thereof before the Recorder's Court of said city, be punished by a fine not exceeding two hundred dollars, and imprisonment for a period not exceeding three months, or either, at the discretion of the Court, and may moreover be held to bail for good behavior.

Riot, disturbance, insulting language, conduct, &c.

SEC. 2. Any person who shall make, aid, countenance or assist in making any noise, riot, disturbance or improper diversion, who shall be guilty of *any indecent, immoral or insulting conduct, language or behavior*, in the streets or elsewhere in said city, and all persons who shall collect in bodies or crowds in said city for unlawful purposes, to the annoyance or disturbance of the citizens or travelers, shall for each offence, on conviction before the said Recorder's Court, be liable to the punishment mentioned in the foregoing section.

Duty of Marshal and Constable.

SEC. 3. The Marshal or any Constable of this city may arrest all such offenders as are before mentioned, and bring them forthwith before any member of the Common Council, who may either discharge the same, or on the oath of one credible witness, commit such offenders to the county jail, unless they shall enter into a recognizance with one or more sufficient sureties, in a sum not exceeding five hundred dollars, conditioned that such offender or offenders shall be and appear before the Recorder's Court at the next ensuing term thereof, to do and receive what shall be then and there required by said Court, and shall be of good behavior and keep the peace in the meantime; and if from any reason, no member of the Common Council can be found immediately after such arrest as aforesaid, such offender or offenders shall be committed for safe keeping, until some one member of the Common Council be enabled to attend to the case.

CHAPTER XLV.

To Punish Drunken and Disorderly Persons, Vagrants, &c.

Punishment of vagrants, &c.

SECTION 1. That all persons who are common prostitutes, vagrants, mendicant street beggars, and drunken or disorderly persons, shall, upon conviction thereof, be punished by fine not to exceed one hundred dollars, or by imprisonment not to exceed ninety days, or by both, in the discretion of the Court.

Persons convicted of vagrancy may be ordered to find security to keep the peace.

SEC. 2. Any person convicted under the preceding section, may, in addition to the punishment fixed in said section, or in lieu thereof, be ordered by the court to enter into a recognizance, with sufficient sureties, for his or her good behavior for the period of one year, and in default of said recognizance being found, said person may be committed to jail until the same is found, or until he or she is discharged by due course of law: *Provided, always,* That no person committed under this section shall remain in prison a longer period than three months from the time of commitment; or, if sentenced to imprisonment under the first section of this ordinance, then said three months shall be counted from and after the expiration of said imprisonment.

What deemed a breach of recognizance.

SEC. 3. The commission of any of the acts which would constitute the person so bound an offender under section first of this ordinance, shall be deemed a breach of the condition of said recognizance.

CHAPTER XLVI.

Relative to the Peace and Quiet of Churches.

Persons not to obstruct public worship.

SECTION 1. That during the time of divine worship in any church or place of worship in said city, upon the Sunday, no person shall be guilty of any loud or boisterous talking, laughing or noise in the public streets of said city within the distance of half a block of said church or place of worship; no persons shall collect and stand in crowds in the streets in front of said church or place of worship, or upon the steps, in the doorways, or on the walks leading to said church or place of worship; no person shall, in the public streets, within the distance of half a block of any church or place of worship, or in the doorways, or on the steps or walks leading to said church or place of worship, use any indecent language, fight, scuffle, or create any disturbance in the presence or hearing of any person or persons going to or from said church or place of worship; and any person or persons who shall violate any of the provisions of this ordinance shall be punished by a fine not exceeding one hundred dollars, or by imprisonment not to exceed three months, or by both said fine and imprisonment, in the discretion of the Court.

How punished.

CHAPTER XLVII.

To prohibit and prevent Riots, Routs, Disorderly Noises, Disturbance and Assemblage, and the Crying of Goods.

Persons guilty of riot how punished.

SECTION 1. That any person or persons who shall be guilty of any riot, rout, disorderly noise or assemblage in the public streets, or in any place within said city, shall, on conviction thereof, be punished by fine not to exceed five hundred dollars, or by imprisonment in the county jail not to exceed two years.

Crying of goods prohibited in streets.

SEC. 2. Any person who shall openly cry any goods within the public streets of said city, shall be fined ten dollars, or punished by ten days' imprisonment in the county jail for each and every offence.

CHAPTER XLVIII.

To Prohibit and Prevent in the Streets or elsewhere, Indecent Exposure of Person.

Indecent exposure of person prohibited.

SECTION 1. That any person who shall make an indecent exposure of his or her person in the public streets, or elsewhere, of said city, shall, on conviction thereof, be punished by a fine not to exceed five hundred dollars, or by imprisonment for a period not to exceed two years.

CHAPTER XLIX.

To Prohibit and Prevent the Show, Sale, or Exhibition for Sale of Indecent or Obscene Pictures, &c.

Obscene books, pictures, &c.

SECTION 1. That any person who shall show, sell, or exhibit for the purpose of sale, any indecent or obscene pictures, drawings, engravings, paintings and books, or pamphlets, or who shall make any indecent or obscene exhibition or show of any kind, in the public streets or elsewhere, of said city, shall, on conviction thereof, be fined not to exceed five hundred dollars, or by imprisonment not to exceed a period of two years.

CHAPTER L.

Relative to Houses of Ill Fame and other Disorderly Houses and Places.

SECTION 1. Every person who shall, within the limits of the city of Detroit, keep a house of ill fame, or of assignation, resorted to for the purpose of prostitution or lewdness, shall be punished by a fine not to exceed five hundred dollars, or by imprisonment not to exceed two years.

SEC. 2. Every person who shall keep a house for the resort of common prostitutes, shall be punished by a fine not to exceed five hundred dollars, or by imprisonment not to exceed two years.

SEC. 3. Every person who shall keep a disorderly house or disorderly grocery, in said city, shall be punished by a fine not to exceed five hundred dollars, or by imprisonment not to exceed two years.

SEC. 4. Every person who shall demise or let any house or premises within said city, for the purpose of being kept or used as a house of ill fame, a house of assignation, disorderly house, or disorderly grocery, or who shall willfully permit any house belonging to him or her to be used or occupied for the purpose of a house of ill fame, house of assignation, disorderly house, or disorderly grocery, shall be punished by a fine not to exceed five hundred dollars, or by imprisonment not to exceed two years.

SEC. 5. Every person who shall commit, or suffer to be committed, in any house, premises, room or buildings occupied by him or her,

TITLE VIII. CHAPTER 51.

any noise, rioting, fighting, revelry or drunkenness calculated to disturb the neighbors, shall be punished by a fine not to exceed one hundred dollars, or by imprisonment not to exceed six months.

SEC. 6. Chapter forty-six of the Revised Ordinances of the year 1855, is hereby repealed.

CHAPTER LI.

Relative to Injuries to Public Property.

Punishment for injury to public property.

SECTION 1. If any person shall destroy, deface, impair, injure or wantonly force open any gate or door, or in any way whatsoever destroy, injure or deface any part of the State capitol building, or the appurtenances, fences, trees or fixtures thereunto belonging or appertaining, the city magazine, hospital, city hall, market houses, water works, water pipes, water screws, hydrants, or any fixtures appertaining to the hydraulic works, weigh scales, street lamps and posts, public wharves, fire engine houses, fire apparatus, public grave yards or trees growing therein, or any grave, tomb or fence around either of them, sidewalks or crosswalks in any street, or any shade or ornamental trees in any street, or any other property whatever, of the State of Michigan, the county of Wayne, or the corporation of the city of Detroit, within the limits of said city, he, she or they so offending, shall forfeit and pay for every such offence a fine not exceeding one hundred dollars and costs of prosecution, together with the expense of repairing the property so injured: *Provided*, That when the injury is accidental, no further fine shall be imposed than the amount of the costs of prosecution and the expense of making such repair.

Private property.

SEC. 2. If any of said property should be owned by individuals, it shall nevertheless be deemed, for the purposes of this chapter, the property of the corporation of said city.

Punishment for using property of the fire department.

SEC. 3. Any person or persons who shall hereafter be guilty of using for any private purposes whatever, any of the fixtures, apparatus, ladders or other property attached or belonging to any of the fire engines, hose or hook and ladder companies of the city of Detroit, without due permission for that purpose first had and obtained of the Chief Engineer, or some one in charge of said property, shall, on conviction thereof in the Recorder's Court, be fined in a sum not exceeding fifty dollars and costs of prosecution, together with the expense of repairing said property, if the same shall in any manner be injured by such unlawful use.

Punishment for injuries to gas and gas lights.

SEC. 4. Any person who shall, without lawful authority, light or extinguish any of the public gas lamps of said city, or who shall in any way change, alter, or turn the stop cock, or any fixture belonging thereto; or who shall break, injure or tarnish any of said lamps, or the posts on which they are erected, shall for each and every offence pay a penalty not exceeding fifty dollars and the costs of prosecution, together with the expense of repairing the property so injured: *Provided*, That when such breaking or injury is accidental, no further fine shall be imposed than the amount of the costs of prosecution and the expense of making such repair.

Penalty.

Duty of officers.

SEC. 5. It shall be the special duty of the Marshal and all the Constables of said city, to make complaint of all violations of this chapter.

CHAPTER LII.

Relative to Injuries to Reservoirs.

Punishment for injuring public reservoirs.

SECTION 1. Any person who shall injure any public reservoir, or who shall break or enter the same, and draw off, or cause to be removed, any of the water therefrom, except in case of fire, or unless duly authorized by the Common Council of said city, or by the Chief Engineer of the Fire Department, (except in case of inspection of fire engines,) shall forfeit and pay a sum not to exceed one hundred dollars, on complaint and conviction in the Recorder's Court of the said offence.

CHAPTER LIII.

Relative to a Night Watch.

Mayor may organize a watch.

SECTION 1. The Mayor of the city is hereby vested with full power and authority to establish and organize a Night Watch, in and for said city; and for that purpose he may appoint as many discreet

TITLE VIII. CHAPTER 53.

and suitable persons as, in his opinion, the public safety may require. The persons appointed as aforesaid, shall, before entering on the performance of their duties, take an oath or affirmation that they will faithfully and honestly discharge the duties of their office, to the best of their ability.

Duties of watch.

SEC. 2. The members of said watch, and each of them, are hereby authorized, and it shall be their duty, between the hours of nine o'clock at night, and the dawn of the succeeding morning, to apprehend any and every person who shall be reasonably suspected of having committed any crime or misdemeanor, or who shall be detected by either of the members of said watch in the violation of any of the ordinances of said city, or of an intent to commit any crime or misdemeanor, and to detain such person until morning; and thereafter, it shall be the duty of such watch to report all persons so apprehended to the Marshal of said city, whó shall thereupon have the custody of all such persons, until discharged by due course of law.

Powers of watchmen.

SEC. 3. That the said watch and every member thereof, shall have power and authority, on reasonable ground of suspicion, during the hours or period of watch aforesaid, to enter in a peaceable manner, or if resisted, (after demand made,) with force, into any house, store, shop, grocery or other building whatever in said city, in which any person or persons may be suspected to be for unlawful purposes, and if any person or persons shall be found therein guilty of any crime or misdemeanor, or who may be reasonably suspected thereof, the said watch to apprehend and keep in custody any such person or persons, in manner as hereinbefore prescribed.

All persons to assist watchmen, when.

SEC. 4. It shall be the duty of all persons in said city, when called upon by any member of said watch, promptly to aid and assist him in the execution of his duties, and if any person shall neglect or refuse to give such aid and assistance, he shall, on conviction, forfeit a sum not exceeding one hundred dollars and costs of prosecution.

Duty of Marshal.

SEC. 5. It shall be the duty of the Marshal of said city, to bring such persons apprehended by said watch before the proper authority, for examination, within a reasonable time; and all persons who shall resist, or in any manner interfere with the members of said watch in the discharge of their duties, shall, on conviction, forfeit a sum not exceeding one hundred dollars and costs of prosecution.

SEC. 6. The Mayor shall have power to remove from office any member of the watch, when, in his opinion, there shall be just cause therefor.

Watchmen may be removed.

SEC. 7. All persons apprehended by said night watch, in the performance of their aforesaid duties, shall be confined in a room in the City Hall, provided for that purpose, during the night in which said person or persons shall be apprehended, subject to the custody and control of said Marshal, whose duty it shall be to take such person or persons, for the purpose of examination, during the morning succeeding their arrest, before the Mayor or Recorder, or, in their absence, one of the Aldermen of said city, who shall, as conservator of the peace of said city, attend at the City Council room, at nine o'clock A. M. of each and every day, except Sunday, during the continuance of said watch, for the purpose of hearing such examination: *Provided*, That persons so apprehended during any Saturday night, shall, on the following morning, be committed to the county jail to be examined as aforesaid, on the Monday following.

What to be done with persons arrested.

CHAPTER LIV.

Relative to Process and Proceedings in the Recorder's Court, and to the Recovery of Fines.

SECTION 1. That upon complaint on oath or affirmation being made to the Clerk of the Recorder's Court, that any person has violated any of the laws or ordinances of said city, the Clerk shall issue a *capias ad respondeudum*, unless a summons be specially prescribed for the arrest of such person, and shall be returnable any day in the present or ensuing term of said Court.

When process may be issued from the Recorder's Court

SEC. 2. Before issuing such process, the Clerk may, if he shall deem it necessary, require the complainant to enter into a bond, with sufficient surety, to the city of Detroit, conditioned for the appearance of the complainant at the term of the Recorder's Court at which such process shall be made returnable, to give evidence against the person or persons complained of by him; and if upon trial the defendant shall be discharged, that the complainant shall pay the costs of prosecution, if so ordered by the said Court.

When security for costs may be required.

SEC. 3. It shall be the duty of the Marshal or Constoble to whom

TITLE VIII. CHAPTER 54.

Who to execute process.

the writ shall be directed, to arrest the defendant therein named if he be found, who may give bail for his appearance at the time such writ shall be returnable, and in default thereof the officer shall take him before any member of the Common Council, who may commit, let to bail, or discharge the defendant, according to his discretion.

Bond upon arrest.

SEC. 4. The bail required in the preceding section, shall be by bond payable to the city of Detroit, with at least one sufficient surety, in a sum not less than fifty dollars, and not more than double the amount of the penalty provided in the by-law or ordinance which may be violated, and shall be conditioned for the due appearance of the defendant before the Recorder's Court at the time such writ shall be returnable, and that the defendant shall comply with the judgment of the Recorder's Court, and not depart without leave, and in the mean time, keep the peace towards all the good people of said city: *Provided*, That if such bail should be insufficient or irresponsible, the officer taking the same shall be liable in an action of debt for the amount thereof, to be recovered in the name of the corporation.

Execution to issue against body, goods and real estate.

SEC. 5. Executions returnable at the next term, may issue upon any judgment of the said Court, againt the body, goods and chattels of the defendant, or party prosecuted, (unless such party be in actual custody for the offence on which judgment was rendered,) for the amount of such fine and the costs of prosecution, which execution may be levied upon the goods and chattels or body of such party, and all goods and chattels so levied upon, shall be sold in the same manner in all respects that personal property is directed by the laws of this State to be sold, except that six days' previous notice of sale shall be sufficient, and the officer levying the same shall return the execution at the next term of the Recorder's Court, with his doings thereon. And if such execution be returned unsatisfied in whole or in part, an execution may be issued against the real estate of such defendant, which shall be executed according to the laws of this State.

When complainant to pay costs.

SEC. 6. If in any trial it shall appear to the Court that the complaint was willful or malicious, or without probable cause, or if the complainant does not appear and testify in the cause, the Court may order and adjudge the complainant (and if he has entered into a bond as required by this ordinance, then against him and his surety,) to pay the costs of such prosecution, and thereupon an execution as in other cases, shall issue for the same.

Constable and Marshal's returns.

SEC. 7. The Marshal and Constables, once in each month, and whenever it can be done, at least three days prior to the term of the Recorder's Court, shall return to the Clerk of said Court all process issued out of said Court, with their doings in each case endorsed thereon, and shall also at such times pay over all moneys collected by them in pursuance of such process, to the City Attorney. And if any such officer shall neglect or refuse to comply with the provisions of this section, or shall knowingly do any other act inconsistent with the just and faithful discharge of his duties, he shall, on conviction, be liable to pay a penalty not exceeding one hundred dollars, and costs of prosecution.

Clerk to report monthly to Council.

SEC. 8. The Clerk shall once in each month make a report to the Common Council of all the particulars and business of the Recorder's Court—the number of persons tried, and the amount of fines and costs of each term, and the amount collected and paid into the hands of the City Attorney; and he shall immediately pay over to the City Treasurer all moneys by him received belonging to the corporation, together with all witness' or jurors' fees on hand, and shall exhibit the receipts of said Treasurer for such moneys.

Penalty for obstructing officers.

SEC. 9. If any person or persons knowingly or willfully obstruct, resist, or oppose the Marshal or any of the Constables of said city, or other person or persons duly authorized in serving or attempting to serve any writ or process, rule or order issued out of said Recorder's Court, or while executing or carrying into effect any order, rule or determination of the Common Council of said city, or shall resist or impede any person duly authorized, or any member of the Common Council of said city, in the performance of any of their duties or powers, or if any person shall aid or assist any person legally in custody, to escape, or conceal him after the escape, every person offending in the premises, shall, on conviction before said Recorder's Court, be punished by fine not exceeding one hundred dollars and costs.

Duty of officers when it is not convenient to bring prisoner before Recorder, Alderman, &c.

SEC. 10. If any officer shall arrest any person, at a time that may be inconvenient to bring him before any proper officer for an examination, the officer making the arrest may place such person in the custody of the Jailer of the county of Wayne, and within fifteen hours thereafter, he shall bring him before some member of the Common Council for examination, and if such officer shall neglect to comply with the requirements of this section, he shall be liable to pay all the expenses of keeping such prisoner in jail: *Provided*, That if the said period of fifteen hours shall terminate on the Sabbath day, said examination shall be had during the forenoon of the next ensuing Monday.

Duty of jailor.

SEC. 11. The keeper of the jail of the county of Wayne shall not permit or suffer any person committed by virtue of a process of the Recorder's Court, or other authority of said city, to leave or depart said jail without the permission of some member of the Common Council, or the City Attorney, under the penalty of a sum not exceeding one hundred dollars, and costs of prosecution.

CHAPTER LV.

To establish Fees in the Recorder's Court.

Fees of Marshals, jurors, witnesses, &c

SECTION 1. For the following services performed in the Recorder's Court of the city of Detroit, in cases authorized by law, officers, witnesses and jurors shall be allowed and receive the fees in this ordinance directed.

SEC. 2. Each Marshal and Assistant Marshal shall be allowed and receive for

Serving warrant.

Serving a warrant or other process for the arrest of any person, twenty-five cents.

Serving subpœna.

Serving a subpœna for a defendant, thirteen cents for each witness, to be paid by said defendant.

For every mile actually and necessarily traveled beyond the city limits, in serving process, six cents.

Jurors' fees.

SEC. 3. Each juror, except talesmen, shall be entitled to and receive the sum of one dollar for each day's attendance upon said Court.

Talesmen's.

Each talesman summoned and acting as a juror in said Court, shall be entitled to and receive the sum of twenty-five cents for each case in which he shall act, unless the time he shall serve shall be equal to one day or more, in which case he shall receive the same sum per day as is allowed to regular jurors.

SEC. 4. In all cases where any person or party shall be ordered to pay the costs of a prosecution of said Court, the sum to be taxed as costs shall be the sum of five dollars, to be paid into the City Treasury.

When parties ordered to pay costs of prosecution, to be taxed $5, to be paid into Treasury

SEC. 5. It shall not be necessary to tender or to pay a fee to a witness subpœnaed on the part of the prosecution or defence in said Court.

Witness' fees not necessary in Recorder's Court.

SEC. 6. Officers serving any process for a defendant in said Court shall be entitled to demand and receive their fees in advance.

Officers to receive their fees in advance.

SEC. 7. Once in every month, the Clerk of said Court shall give to each officer and juror of said Court a statement, certified by said Clerk, of all services rendered by said officer or juror.

Clerk to give monthly certificates of services.

SEC. 8. The person holding said certificate may present the same to the Controller, who shall audit, and, if correct, allow, and draw his warrant for the amount of the same, in the same manner as in other accounts: *Provided, always*, That in the case of jurors, before auditing their claims, the said Controller shall satisfy himself that they have not been paid, and are not entitled to be paid for the services charged in said statement, by the county of Wayne.

Controller to draw his warrant for same as other accounts.

Proviso.

CHAPTER LVI.

To establish Fees of Constables in the Recorder's Court.

SECTION 1. That the following sums shall be paid to Constables of the city of Detroit, for services in the Recorder's Court, that is to say:

Constables' fees.

For serving every writ, fifty cents for each person taken into custody;

For each defendant taken to prison on final commitment, thirteen cents;

For serving subpœnas and writs without the borders of the city, and within the county of Wayne, thirteen cents for the first mile and six cents for each other mile necessarily traveled in serving said writ or subpœna;

Subpœnas.

For serving subpœnas, thirteen cents for each person subpœnaed;

For arresting parties without process, fifty cents for each person

Arrests.

TITLE IX. CHAPTER 57.

arrested: *Provided*, That no additional charge shall be made for serving a warrant upon any party so arrested.

Accounts to contain the names of persons arrested, certificate of Clerk and Attor'ny, before payment by Controller.

SEC. 2. The Controller shall audit no bill or account for services rendered under this ordinance, save under the following conditions, that is to say: Said bill or account shall contain the names of all persons who have been arrested, subpœnaed or taken to prison, the offence for which arrested, and the case in which subpœnaed, and shall be certified to by the Clerk of the Recorder's Court, under the seal of said Court, and shall further be accompanied by a certificate from the City Attorney that the persons subpœnaed were subpœnaed on behalf of the people on his order, and wherever mileage is charged, the person claiming the same shall, if required by the Controller, make oath to the correctness of the charge.

Bills—when to be rendered and how paid.

SEC. 3. All bills or accounts for fees under this ordinance shall be rendered to the City Controller on the last Friday of each month and shall, before payment by him, be submitted to the Common Council, and shall only be paid upon their direction, upon being approved by a committee to whom they shall be referred for examination.

SEC. 4. This ordinance shall be in force from and after ten days after the passage thereof.

TITLE NINE.

OF STRAY ANIMALS.

CHAPTER LVII.

Relative to Pound Masters and Public Pounds.

Location of pounds.

SECTION 1. There shall be one or more public pounds in said city, in such place as the Common Council shall designate and provide.

Term of office of Pound Masters.

SEC. 2. The Common Council of said city shall appoint one or more Pound Masters in and for said city, who shall hold their office during the pleasure of the Council, who shall take and file the oath required of officers by the city charter, and give bonds to the city, with two sufficient sureties, in the sum of five hundred dollars, and conditioned as is prescribed for official bonds by said charter.

Keepers to live near pounds.

SEC. 3. Said pound keepers shall have the charge of, and live at or near the public pounds.

Cattle not to run at large.

SEC. 4. No cattle, horses, asses, mules, swine, sheep, goats, geese, or domestic fowls, shall run at large in the streets, or elsewhere in said city within the following limits, that is to say: within the city limits.

Cattle running at large to be impounded.

SEC. 5. Any horses, cattle, asses, mules, swine, sheep, goats, geese or domestic fowls running at large within said limits, and each and every of them, may be impounded in said public pounds.

Who may impound.

SEC. 6. Any officer of said city, and any other person, and minors under eighteen years of age, may take up and drive to the public pound any of the animals mentioned in the preceding section, found so running at large.

Duties of keeper.

SEC. 7. It shall be the duty of the pound keepers to receive and safely keep and sustain in the public pound any of said animals so as aforesaid taken up and driven to said pounds.

Keeper to keep register

SEC. 8. It shall be the duty of the pound keepers to register in a book, to be kept for the purpose, the time when any animal was received into the public pound, the name and residence of the person by whom said animal was taken up, and the place where said animal was found running at large. He shall provide necessary sustenance for all animals impounded, and shall, upon Wednesday and Saturday of each week, sell at public auction any animal which has been impounded in said pound three days, and is unclaimed by any person, or whose owner refuses to pay the fees, costs and charges of impounding and keeping said animal, first giving forty-eight hours' written or printed notice of the sale of said animal, which notice shall state, as near as may be, a description of said animal, the person by whom, and the place where, it was taken up, and the time when it was impounded, which notice shall be posted in four different places in said city, to wit: one at the City Hall, another at the Post Office, another in the division of the city where said animal was found running at large, and another at the public pound; and said sale shall be held at the public pounds.

Days of sale, after notice.

Notices, when to be posted.

Owner may redeem before sale.

SEC. 9. Any person owning any animal impounded in the public pounds, may redeem said animal any time before it is sold, by pay-

17

ing to the pound keeper the costs, charges and fees hereinafter provided, and by proving to his satisfaction the ownership of said animal.

Costs and charges.

SEC. 10. The following costs, charges and fees shall be demanded by the pound keeper, and shall be paid by the person claiming any animal, before said animal shall be redeemed, to wit: for the sustenance of each head of cattle, each horse, ass or mule, twenty-five cents per day; for the sustenance of each swine, sheep, goat, goose or domestic fowl, twelve cents per day; for receiving and discharging or selling each horse, ass, mule, swine or head of cattle, one dollar and fifty cents; for receiving and discharging or selling any sheep, goat, goose or domestic fowl, twenty-five cents.

Pound keeper to render statement to Controller.

SEC. 11. The pound keepers shall, on Monday of each week, render to the Controller a sworn statement of all moneys received by them during the preceding week, and shall, at the same time, show to said Controller a receipt from the Treasurer of said city, for said moneys.

Pound keepers to procure supplies.

SEC. 12. The pound keepers shall procure all supplies needed for the sustenance of animals in the public pound, and shall certify to all bills for such supplies, which bills shall be audited by the City Controller, who shall, upon finding them correct, draw his warrant for the amount thereof.

Controller to keep account of receipts and disbursements.

SEC. 13. The Controller shall keep a separate account of all moneys received from, and all moneys paid out for, the public pounds, and the sustenance of animals therein, and shall report the state of said account to the Common Council, in his annual report.

Salary of Pound keepers.

SEC. 14. The pound keepers shall receive in full for their services the sum of one dollar and fifty cents per day for each and every day they act as pound keepers.

Pound keepers to pay fine for illegal acts.

SEC. 15. If said pound keepers shall refuse to receive into the public pound any animal which may legally be impounded therein, or if they shall receive into and keep in the pounds, or sell as pound keepers, or receive any fees, costs or charges for any animal not legally liable to be impounded, they shall, on conviction thereof, be punished by a fine not exceeding twenty-five dollars, or by fifteen days' imprisonment.

Penalty for impounding animals illegally.

SEC. 16. If any person shall take up and carry to the public pounds any animal not legally liable to be impounded therein, said person shall be punished by a fine of five dollars for each and every offence.

Moneys received to be applied to sustain the pounds.

SEC. 17. All moneys received into the city treasury from the pound masters, and all fines collected under this act, shall be placed in and constitute a fund to be used as far as possible for the support of all the expenses of the public pounds, save the salary of the pound keepers.

Owner to receive surplus of sale after defraying expenses.

SEC. 18. Whenever any animal is sold under the provisions of this ordinance, and the amount for which said animal is sold exceeds the amount of the costs, fees, and charges herein allowed for receiving and discharging or selling said animal, and for the sustenance of said animal, the owner of said animal may, upon satisfying the City Treasurer of the ownership of said animal, receive the excess of said fees, costs and charges from said Treasurer, on giving to said Treasurer proper vouchers therefor.

Penalty for obstructing persons driving animals.

SEC. 19. Each and every person who shall hinder, delay or obstruct any person or persons in driving to the pounds any animal or animals, beast or beasts, liable to be impounded in the city pounds, shall, for each and every hindrance, delay or obstruction, and for each and every person delayed, pay a fine of not less than ten dollars, nor more than twenty dollars.

Penalty for breaking open the pound.

SEC. 20. If any person or persons shall break open, or in any manner, directly or indirectly, aid or assist in breaking open any city pound, said person or persons shall severally, on conviction thereof before the Recorder's Court of said city, be punished by a fine not exceeding five dollars and the costs of prosecution, and imprisonment for the period of five days, or either, in the discretion of said Court.

Pound keeper to give a certificate of the facts to Controller.

SEC. 21. The pound keeper shall give to each and every person bringing an animal to the pound, a certificate of the fact that said person did, upon the day named in the certificate, bring said animal to the pound, and said person, upon presenting said certificate to the Controller, shall be entitled to receive from the City Treasurer for each head of cattle, horse, ass, mule or swine so impounded and certified to, the sum of seventy-five cents; and for each sheep, goat, goose or domestic fowl, the sum of ten cents.

CHAPTER LVIII.

Relative to Pound Keepers, Fence Viewers, &c.

Duties of pound keepers.

SECTION 1. Pound Keepers shall have and exercise the same power, duties and privileges, and be subject to the same restrictions, so far as the said power, duties, privileges and restrictions are consistent with chapter fifty-seven of these ordinances, and the laws of the State prescribe relative to the keeper of a public pound.

Fence viewers.

SEC. 2. The Overseer of Highways of said city shall have and exercise the same powers, duties and privileges, and be subject to the same restrictions and penalties, as the laws of this State prescribe relative to Fence Viewers.

Laws of this State applicable to pounds may be enforced in Recorder's Court.

SEC. 3. Every provision of the law of this State relative to Pound Keepers thereof, Fence Viewers, stray cattle or beasts in the pound, are hereby adopted, and all violations of the same shall be prosecuted in the Recorder's Court of said city.

CHAPTER LIX.

Relative to Dogs.

Dogs may be taxed.

SECTION 1. Every person residing in this city, owning or having in his possession, or suffering to be kept on his or her premises any dog, shall be liable to be assessed and pay for the same, the following taxes: for one dog, the sum of fifty cents per annum, (commencing on the first Monday in April,) for every additional dog, two dollars, to be assessed and collected in the same manner as taxes upon personal property in said city.

Owners of dogs to report to assessors.

SEC. 2. Every person residing in this city owning or having in his or her possession, or suffering to be kept on his or her premises, any dog, shall, on or before the third Monday in March, in each year, report to the City Assessor the name and description of every dog so owned or possessed by him, and shall put upon the neck of every dog a metal strap or collar, on which shall be engraved in legible letters the name of the owner. Any person neglecting any of the provisions of this section, shall forfeit the penalty of five dollars for every neglect.

SEC. 3. It shall be lawful for any person to shoot, or otherwise kill or destroy, any dog found running at large in this city, contrary to the requirements of the preceding section. Dogs may be killed.

SEC. 4. It shall be the duty of the City Assessor to keep a record of the name and description of all dogs reported to him as aforesaid, together with the name and description of any other dog which he shall ascertain at the time of making his annual assessment, and return the same to the City Clerk, who shall deliver the same to the Collector. Assessor to keep register of dogs, &c.

SEC. 5. No slut or bitch shall be kept, or allowed to be kept, or remain within the limits of the city, and such as may be found or shall be seen going at large within the limits aforesaid, shall be liable to be killed by the Marshal or any other person. All sluts and bitches shall be killed.

SEC. 6. No person shall be allowed to keep, or suffer to run at large, any dog or slut of vicious or ferocious character or disposition, under penalty for each offence, not exceeding ten dollars, and the City Marshal or any other person is hereby required to kill, or cause any such dog or bitch to be killed, if found running at large, or that an injury has been wantonly caused by any such dog or slut to any person. Vicious dogs may be killed

SEC. 7. It shall not be lawful for any dog, slut or bitch, to run at large within the limits of the city of Detroit, unless muzzled, as hereinafter provided for. Dogs to be muzzled.

SEC. 8. No dog, slut or bitch shall be allowed to run at large within the limits of said city unless muzzled with a good and sufficient muzzle, rendering it impossible for such dog, slut or bitch to do any mischief by biting any person or animal. Dogs running at large to be muzzled.

SEC. 9. It shall be the duty of the Marshal to kill every dog, slut or bitch found running at large within the limits of said city, contrary to the provisions of the preceding sections. Marshal to kill dogs, when.

SEC. 10. It shall be lawful for the Marshal, when the safety of the citizens shall require the vigorous enforcement of this chapter, to employ such number of discreet persons to kill all dogs, sluts and bitches as shall be found running at large *unmuzzled*, or with defective muzzles: *Provided*, The expense shall not exceed twenty-five cents for every dog, slut or bitch so killed. May employ assistant dog killers.

SEC. 11. The operation of the four preceding sections may be

TITLE X. CHAPTER 60.

Suspension of four preceding sections, when.

suspended at any time when the public safety shall, in the opinion of the Common Council, authorize such suspension.

TITLE TEN.

OF FERRIES, HACKS, AND DRAYS.

CHAPTER LX.

Relative to Ferries.

Ferries to be licensed.

Penalty.

SECTION 1. That no person shall use or keep any ferry or boat for transporting for hire across the river Detroit, any persons, cattle, carriages or other matter whatever, from within the limits of the city of Detroit, without having previously obtained a license from the Common Council of the said city, under a penalty not exceeding twenty-five dollars for each offence, to be recovered for the use of the said city with costs.

License how obtained and recognizance

SEC. 2. Each license shall be for the term of one year, and shall issue only on the petition or recommendation in writing, of at least twelve respectable freeholders of the said city, stating that a ferry is needed at the place therein designated, and that the applicant is a person suitable to keep the same, and if the prayer of such petition be granted, such applicant shall, before receiving such license, pay to the Treasurer of said city such sum as the Common Council shall deem reasonable for such license, and shall also enter into a recognizance to the city of Detroit, by himself, in the sum of one hundred dollars, and two sufficient sureties in the sum of fifty dollars each, conditioned that he shall faithfully keep in complete repair one or more sufficient and safe boats and scows as may be necessary for the safe conveyance of persons, wagons, carriages, cattle, horses and all other articles necessary to be transported, and shall, at all times, when the said river is passable, give due attendance with a sufficient number of hands to work and manage said boats and scows at the said ferry, during such hours in each day and night, and at such prices or rates for ferriage as shall be, from time to time, prescribed by the said

Common Council, which recognizance shall be taken and remain in the Clerk's office of said city; and upon the perfection thereof and payment of the aforesaid sum, a license for such right of ferriage shall be issued to the said applicant.

Number of ferries allowed.

SEC. 3. The granting of any license for the aforesaid purpose shall not be deemed to deprive the Common Council of the power to grant as many more as they may think proper, and no greater fee or payment shall be demanded for ferriage at any time other than as fixed by law, under a penalty of not more than fifty dollars for each offence, with costs of suit, and such penalty shall be independent of and in addition to any remedy on the aforesaid recognizance.

Illegal fees.

Penalty.

Time of attendance on ferry.

SEC. 4. Each ferry keeper shall attend his ferry from sunrise in the morning until sundown in the evening, and shall be liable to be deprived of his license by the Common Council in case of failure or omission to comply with the directions of this chapter, or the conditions of his recognizance. And such ferry keeper during the period aforesaid, when such river is passable, shall not detain any person, or any person with his goods, cattle or other property necessary and proper to be transported, more than fifteen minutes from the time application is made by such person to be ferried over said river with his goods and other property aforesaid; and for every such offence, he shall forfeit a sum not exceeding twenty-five dollars and costs of prosecution.

No person to be detained.

Penalty.

Ferry place not to be changed.

SEC. 5. No ferry keeper shall remove his ferry to any other place in said city than that designated in his said application for license, without the permission of the Common Council; nor shall any ferry keeper at any time, permit any gaming for money or other value, or suffer any drunkenness, quarreling, fighting, blasphemy, or any rude, disorderly or immoral conduct, on any boat or scow engaged or used by him in ferrying said river. And any person offending in the premises, on conviction, shall forfeit a sum not exceeding fifty dollars for each offence, and be liable to have his license suppressed and declared void.

Gaming, &c., prohibited.

Penalty.

Rates of fare.

SEC. 6. The rates of ferriage shall be as follows, to wit: from the first day of April to the first day of November in each year, for each person twelve and a half cents; for each horse twenty-five cents; for one horse and carriage and persons thereto belonging, not exceeding two, fifty cents; for a carriage and two horses, and persons as

TITLE X. CHAPTER 61.

last aforesaid, seventy-five cents; for every additional horse, eighteen and three-fourths cents; for each head of horned cattle, twenty-five cents, and for each sheep or hog, six cents. And from the first day of November to the first day of April following, for each person, twelve and a half cents; for each horse, thirty-seven and a half cents; for each horse and carriage and persons thereto belonging, not exceeding two, seventy-five cents; for each carriage and two horses, and persons as last aforesaid, one dollar and twenty-five cents; for each additional horse, twenty-five cents; for each head of horned cattle, thirty-seven and a half cents; and for each sheep or hog, six and a quarter cents.

Keeper to print a list of rates.

SEC. 7. It shall be the duty of every person authorized to keep a ferry within the limits of said city, to cause to be affixed, and at all times to keep, in some conspicuous place near the ferry landing, and in each boat or scow used for the purpose of ferriage, a list of the rates of ferriage; which shall be painted on a board in plain and legible characters, so that it may be seen by the public, and shall be headed thus: "Legal charges for ferriage across the river Detroit, as established by law." And if any person shall neglect or refuse to comply with the provisions of this section, he shall, on conviction, forfeit the sum of five dollars and costs of prosecution, for every day's omission.

CHAPTER LXI.

Relative to Cabs, Hackney Coaches, Omnibuses and Carriages, &c.

Cabs, &c., to be licensed.

SECTION 1. The City Clerk may issue a license under the corporate seal of the city, to any trustworthy person or persons, of the ages of twenty-one years, or upwards, who shall be residents of said city, authorizing such person or persons to keep cabs, hackney coaches, carriages, omnibuses, or other vehicles, for hire, upon such person or persons complying with the provisions of this ordinance, and giving proper security, and upon paying five dollars to the City Treasurer for every cab, hackney coach, carriage, omnibus or other vehicle, authorized to be kept by such license. Such license shall state the number of each cab, coach, carriage, omnibus, or other vehicle allowed to be kept under said license, with the name of the person to whom it is granted, and shall, in all cases, continue in force for the period of one year next ensuing the date thereof. And no person shall keep or use any hackney coach, cab, carriage, omnibus or other vehicle, for hire, in said city of Detroit, without being licensed as aforesaid; and in case any person shall keep or use any such hackney coach, carriage, cab, omnibus or other vehicle, for hire, without having taken out license for that purpose, as aforesaid, he shall, upon conviction of the offence, in the Recorder's Court, pay a fine of ten dollars and costs of prosecution. Penalty.

SEC. 2. Every person to whom a license shall be granted, as provided for in the foregoing section, shall execute a bond to the city of Detroit in the sum of two hundred dollars, with sufficient sureties, to be approved by the City Controller, conditioned that such person will pay all fines, costs, penalties or damages, for which he may become liable on account of the use of any cab, hackney coaches, carriages, omnibuses, or other vehicles kept or used by such person, under his license as aforesaid; and no license shall be of any validity until such bond has been duly executed and filed with the City Clerk. Bond given on license issued.

SEC. 3. The prices which may be charged by the owners or drivers of hackney coaches, cabs, carriages, omnibuses or other vehicles, shall not exceed as follows, viz.: For conveying one person, for each drive less than an hour, twenty-five cents; for conveying two or more persons, for each drive less than one hour, twenty-five cents for each person; for the use of a cab, carriage, hackney coach, or other vehicle, (except an omnibus,) by the hour, to carry not more than four persons inside, at the rate of one dollar per hour: *Provided*, That children between two and twelve years of age shall be conveyed at one-half the foregoing rates; and infants under two years of age shall be carried free, if in charge of any other person. Prices.

SEC. 4. When a cab, carriage, hackney coach, or other vehicle shall be used for a longer time than one hour, the owner or driver thereof shall be entitled to charge and receive from the person or persons using the same, the sum of one dollar for each full hour the same shall have been used; and for fractional parts of an hour he shall only charge and receive at the rate of one dollar per hour, as aforesaid. Price when cab used more than an hour.

SEC. 5. For each trunk carried on any cab, carriage, hackney coach, omnibus or other vehicle, the owner or driver thereof may Price for baggage.

TITLE X. CHAPTER 61.

charge and receive the sum of twelve and one-half cents, and no more: *Provided*, That each person hiring or using any such carriage, cab, omnibus, or other vehicle, shall be allowed to carry thereon any ordinary traveling bag, valise or bundle, weighing less than forty-five pounds, free of all charge.

Rates of fare at night.

SEC. 6. When a cab, carriage, omnibus, hackney coach or other vehicle shall be hired or used between the hours of eleven o'clock in the evening and five o'clock in the morning, the owner or driver thereof shall be entitled to charge and receive one-half more than the rates prescribed in the foregoing section, and no more.

Charge not to exceed amount allowed for an hour, when.

SEC. 7. In no case shall any person, or any number of persons, less than five, be charged for the use of a cab, carriage, hackney coach, or other vehicle, more than the sum allowed for the use thereof, for one hour, unless the same shall be used more than one hour, although the person or persons using the same may have stopped at several places during the time he, she or they may have been using such cab, carriage, hackney coach or other vehicle.

Punishment of cabmen, &c., for what.

SEC. 8. A fine of not less than twenty-five dollars, nor more than one hundred dollars and costs of prosecution, shall be imposed by the Recorder's Court upon the owner or driver of any hackney coach, cab, carriage, omnibus or other vehicle, who shall demand or receive higher or greater prices or rates, for the use of his cab, carriage, hackney coach, omnibus or other vehicle, than those named and fixed by the foregoing sections of this ordinance; and a fine of ten dollars and costs of prosecution shall be imposed by the Recorder's Court upon the owner or driver of the foregoing named vehicles, or any other vehicles used for hire in said city, who shall unreasonably refuse or neglect to convey any person or persons within the bounds of said city, when applied to for that purpose, and being at the time unemployed; and the like fine shall be imposed by said Court upon the owner or driver of either of the foregoing named vehicles, or any other vehicles used for hire in said city, who shall neglect to place upon such vehicle, in a conspicuous place inside, a card, on which shall be legibly printed the number of the license under which such vehicle is used, the name of the owner thereof, and the prices or rates fixed by this ordinance for the use of cabs, hackney coaches, carriages, omnibuses and other vehicles.

SEC. 9. All keepers of livery stables within said city shall pay the sum of five dollars to the City Treasurer for every carriage, cab, or other vehicle which they may at any time place on a public stand, or run as a public conveyance within said city; and all carriages or other vehicles placed by any livery stable keeper on a public stand, shall be regularly numbered, and subject to all the provisions hereinbefore contained relative to rates or prices of conveyance; and in case any livery stable keeper shall place a carriage or other vehicle on a public stand without paying the said sum of five dollars to the City Treasurer, and placing a number on his carriage or other vehicle, he shall, upon conviction of the offence in the Recorder's Court, be fined ten dollars and costs of prosecution.

Livery stables to pay $5 to Treasurer for each vehicle; and subject to provisions of this ordinance.

SEC. 10. No hotel keeper who may keep an omnibus, carriage or other vehicle for the purpose of carrying passengers to and from steamboats and railroad depots, or other plces in said city, shall be permitted to use the same for carrying any person or persons for hire in and through said city, except on taking out a license according to the provisions of section one of this ordinance, and paying the regular fee therefor, and for every violation of the provisions of this section, the person or persons offending, on conviction in the Recorder's Court, shall be fined ten dollars and costs of prosecution.

Hotel keepers to pay licences.

SEC. 11. The Recorder's Court, in its discretion, may order any person or persons found guilty of a violation of any of the provisions of this ordinance, to be imprisoned in the common jail of Wayne county for a term not exceeding ninety days, besides the fines and costs hereinbefore authorized; and the Mayor or any three Aldermen of the city, may at any time revoke the license of any person who shall be found guilty of having violated any of the provisions of this ordinance.

Recorder's Court may order persons violating this ordinance imprisoned, and Mayor or Recorder, or any three Aldermen, may revoke license.

SEC. 12. In all cases where complaints shall be made by a stranger or non-resident of said city for a violation of any of the provisions of this ordinance, and the person or persons complained of shall be found guilty, upon trial in the Recorder's Court, or shall plead guilty, the complainant shall be entitled to receive one-half of the fine imposed upon the person or persons complained of, after the same has been collected and paid to the City Treasurer; and it shall be the duty of the City Treasurer, on receiving such fine, to pay one-half thereof to such complainant, on demand, and take a receipt therefor.

When one-half of fine to go to non-resident complainants.

SEC. 13. All sleighs, cutters or other conveyances used by persons

TITLE X. CHAPTER 61.

Sleighs and cutters subject to provisions of this ordinance.

for hire, within said city, during the season of sleighing, shall be subject to all the provisions of this ordinance in regard to rates or prices of hire for cabs, carriages, hackney coaches, omnibuses or other vehicles.

Clerk to keep register of persons licensed, and of numbers of vehicles.

SEC. 14. The City Clerk shall keep a register of the names of all persons licensed according to the provisions of this ordinance, in which shall be stated the number and date of the license granted to each person, and the number of cabs, carriages, coaches, omnibuses or other vehicles allowed to be kept or used under each license; and at the time of granting each license, the Clerk shall give to the person or persons taking the same, a number for each of the vehicles allowed to be kept by such person or persons, and also enter such number on his register; and every person taking out a license as aforesaid, shall forthwith place, or cause to be placed, in conspicuous figures, on the outside of the door or doors of each vehicle kept or used under such license, the number given him by the City Clerk, as aforesaid; and in case there are no doors to such vehicle, the number shall be placed on both sides of the box of such vehicle, in a conspicuous place. Any person or persons failing to comply with the provisions of this section, on conviction thereof, in the Recorder's Court, shall be fined ten dollars and costs of prosecution. The Mayor may, at any time, in his discretion, revoke such license granted as provided in the preceding sections of this ordinance.

Drivers to be licensed.

SEC. 15. No persons shall drive any cabs, hackney coaches, carriages, omnibuses or other vehicles, licensed to be kept for hire under the first section of this chapter, unless said person shall have been licensed as a public driver, and no person licensed under said first section shall employ any driver who is not licensed, as is required by this section. Any person violating the provisions of this section shall be punished by a fine not to exceed fifty dollars, or by imprisonment not to exceed forty days: *Provided, always*, That this section shall not be construed to prevent persons licensed under the said first section from driving their own vehicles which they have been licensed to keep.

SEC. 16. No person who is not licensed as a driver under the preceding section, or who is not licensed under the said first section, shall manage, take charge of, procure passengers for, or charge or receive moneys for the use of any cab, hackney coach, carriage, omnibus or any other vehicles which are plied for hire within said city; neither shall more than one licensed person occupy the top of, or take charge of, or ride in a hackney coach, carriage, cab, omnibus, or other vehicle, when waiting employment at boats or cars, or when at any time or in any place said hackney coach, cab, carriage, omnibus or other vehicles are in actual use carrying passengers for hire. Any person violating the provisions of this section shall be punished by a fine not to exceed fifty dollars, or by imprisonment not to exceed forty days.

Persons not licensed not to take charge of or solicit passengers, &c., and but one so licensed to occupy hack, &c.

SEC. 17. Drivers shall be licensed by the City Clerk upon presenting to him the written permit of the Mayor and receipt of the City Treasurer for the sum of one dollar, and all licenses issued under this chapter shall be in force until the first day of August ensuing the date of their issuance.

Drivers to have Mayor's permit before being licensed.

SEC. 18. Licenses to drivers may be revoked at any time by the Mayor or Common Council of said city, and no person whose license has been revoked shall be re-licensed without the special consent of the Mayor or Common Council.

Licenses may be revoked.

CHAPTER LXII.

Relative to Stands of Public Carriages, &c.

SECTION 1. That hereafter all hackney coaches, carriages, cabs and other vehicles used for carrying passengers, plying for hire within the limits of the city, shall, while waiting for employment, occupy the following stands and no others, that is to say: The centre of Jefferson avenue, from a point fifteen feet easterly of the east line of Woodward avenue, to a point fifteen feet westerly of the west line of Bates street; the centre of Jefferson avenue from a point fifteen feet westerly of the west line of Woodward Avenue, to a point fifteen feet easterly of the east line of Griswold street; the centre of Woodward avenue, from a point fifteen feet northerly of the north line of Jefferson Avenue, to a point fifteen feet southerly of the south line of Larned street; the centre of Woodward avenue, from a point fifteen feet southerly of the south line of Jefferson avenue, to a point fifteen feet northerly of the north line of Woodbridge street.

Places where cabs, &c., to stand.

SEC. 2. All drays, carts, wagons and other vehicles used for the

TITLE X. CHAPTER 63.

Stands for drays, &c.

transportation of goods, merchandise and other wares, plying for hire within the limits of the city, shall, while waiting for employment, occupy the following stands, and no others, that is to say: The centre of Jefferson avenue, between Griswold street and Third street; the centre of Jefferson avenue, between Bates street and Brush street; the centre of Woodward Avenue, between Larned street and the Campus Martius; the centre of Woodward avenue, between Woodbridge street and the river: *Provided*, That none of the said vehicles shall stand within fifteen feet of any cross street.

Driver to remain on his vehicle.

SEC. 3. The driver of any carriage, cart or other vehicle mentioned in this ordinance, shall, while waiting for employment as aforesaid, remain upon his said vehicle.

Vehicles to occupy centre of streets.

SEC. 4. The said vehicles, while occupying the stands aforesaid, shall stand in the centre of said streets, and in a line parallel with the course of said streets.

Penalty.

SEC. 5. Any person violating any of the provisions of this ordinance, shall, for each offence, upon conviction before the Recorder's Court, forfeit and pay a fine of not more than fifty dollars and costs of prosecution.

CHAPTER LXIII.

Relative to Draymen, Cartmen, Truckmen, Wagoners, &c., &c.

Drays to be licensed.

SECTION 1. No person shall ply any cart, dray, wagon, truck or other vehicle within the limits of said city, for hire, without a license.

Who may be licensed and how.

SEC. 2. No person who has not resided in said city at least six months, shall be licensed as a cartman, drayman, truckman or wagoner, without the special consent of the Common Council; but any person who has resided in said city six months or more, and who shall be deemed by the Mayor or Common Council a proper person, may obtain such license from the City Clerk, by first paying the City Treasurer the sum of one dollar and obtaining his receipt for the same.

Licenses not to be assigned.

SEC. 3. No person, licensed under this ordinance, shall assign his license, or permit any person to drive his wagon, cart, dray, truck o other vehicle, without permission of the Mayor or Common Council.

SEC. 4. Each person having a cart, dray, truck, wagon or other vehicle, licensed as aforesaid, shall cause the number of his license to be conspicuously and distinctly placed upon each side of said cart, dray, truck, wagon, or other vehicle.

Drays, &c., to be numbered.

SEC. 5. The price to be demanded and received by persons licensed as above shall not exceed twenty cents for each load, unless drawn more than one mile, when ten cents additional per mile may be added: *Provided, always*, That it shall be lawful to demand and receive for removing each load of household furniture from one dwelling house to another, the sum of forty cents.

Rates.

SEC. 6. No person shall ask, demand or receive a larger sum than is provided in the foregoing section, for hauling any dray load, cart load, truck load or wagon load, within the limits of said city, unless by previous agreement.

No greater rate to be asked, unless by agreement.

SEC. 7. No cartman, drayman, wagoner, truckman, or the owner or driver of any other vehicle, shall be guilty of any deceit or embezzlement in the execution of his duty, or of cruelty to his own horse, or that of any other person placed in his charge.

Draymen, &c., not to be guilty of embezzlement, &c., or cruelty to animals.

SEC. 8. The Mayor or Common Council may at any time revoke the license of any cartman, drayman, truckman or wagoner, for such cause as he or they may deem sufficient, and no person, whose license is so revoked, shall again obtain a license within twelve months from the date of such revocation, without the special permission of the Council.

Mayor or Common Council may revoke license, for cause.

SEC. 9. All licenses granted under this ordinance shall expire on the first day of August next ensuing the date thereof.

When licenses to expire.

SEC. 10. Any violation of the provisions of this ordinance shall be punished by a fine not to exceed fifty dollars, or an imprisonment of not to exceed three months, or both such fine and imprisonment, in the discretion of the Court.

Penalty for violation of ordinance.

SEC. 11. This ordinance shall take effect and be in force from and after the first day of August next.

TITLE XI.
CHAPTER 64.

TITLE ELEVEN.

OF PLACES OF REFRESHMENT AND RECREATION.

CHAPTER LXIV.

Relative to Ordinaries and Groceries.

Of the internal order of groceries and ordinaries.

SECTION 1. No person or persons who may keep an ordinary, victualing house or grocery, within the limits of the city of Detroit, nor any person employed by, or acting for him or her, shall at any time knowingly permit any gaming for money, or for other value, within his, her or their premises, or suffer any drunkenness, reveling, quarreling, fighting, blasphemy or any other disorderly or immoral conduct, or keep his, her or their establishment open during any part of the Sabbath, or sell any liquors or beverages prohibited by the laws of the State, or keep open any house at any time after half-past ten o'clock at night; any person or persons offending in the premises, on conviction thereof before the Recorder's Court of the city of Detroit, shall forfeit and pay for every such offence, for the use of said city, a sum not exceeding one hundred dollars, with the costs of prosecution.

Duty of Marshal and Constables.

SEC. 2. It shall be the duty of the Marshal and Constables to notice and enquire into all offences under this chapter, and to notify the City Attorney of the same, who, upon such notification, shall cause proceedings against the guilty party or parties to be instituted in the Recorder's Court.

CHAPTER LXV.

Relative to Ball Alleys, Billiard and other Tables.

Keepers of ball alleys, &c., to be licensed.

SECTION 1. No person or persons shall keep, or permit to be kept in his, her or their premises, within the limits of said city, any ball alley, or any billiard table, or other tables for the purpose of playing at any game whatsoever, or to allow any person or persons to play at such alley, or such table or tables, unless the person keeping the same has been previously licensed to do so, by the authority of the Common Council of said city.

License, how obtained.

SEC. 2. It shall be the duty of any person or persons who may be desirous of keeping any ball alley, billiard table or other table, to make application to the Common Council of said city for license; and such license may be granted on paying the sum, and on filing the bond hereinafter required; but no such license shall be granted for a shorter period than three months.

Amount of license, recognizance, &c.

SEC. 3. No person shall receive such license until he shall have paid to the Treasurer of said city such sum as the Common Council may determine for one year, for each and every ball alley, billiard table or other table; the person applying for any such license shall also enter into recognizance to the city of Detroit, himself in the sum of one hundred dollars, with two sufficient sureties, in the sum of fifty dollars, to be taken and acknowledged before the City Clerk, conditioned that such applicant shall well and truly observe and keep all the requirements of this chapter, and shall neither do nor permit to be done anything contrary thereto.

Premises closed when, no gambling, &c.

SEC. 4. No person licensed as aforesaid, shall at any time permit or suffer any gaming for money or other value, within any ball alley or billiard table, or other such establishment kept by him; nor shall any person be guilty of betting or gaming for money or other value therein; nor shall any person so licensed, suffer therein or thereabouts, any drunkenness, quarreling, fighting or any other disorderly conduct, nor keep any such establishment open during any part of the Sabbath, or first day of the week, or after the hour of ten o'clock in the evening, or before the hour of eight o'clock in the forenoon of any day, nor permit to play thereon or thereat, any minor, apprentice or servant, after the parent, guardian, master or mistress of such person shall have notified such keeper not to permit such minor, apprentice or servant to play.

Penalty.

SEC. 5. Any person or persons who shall offend against any of the provisions of this chapter, shall, on conviction thereof, be liable to a fine not exceeding one hundred dollars and costs of prosecution for each offence, and on conviction a second time, the person so licensed, shall be liable to have his license suppressed and annulled.

TITLE XI. CHAPTER 66.

CHAPTER LXVI.

To Prohibit Gaming within the City of Detroit.

All games for money prohibited.

SECTION 1. That any person or persons gaming for money with cards, dice, billiards, nine or ten pin alleys, wheels of fortune, tables, ball alleys, boxes, machines or other instruments or devices of any kind, in any grocery, store, shop, tavern, street, alley, room or any other place within said city, shall be punished, on conviction thereof, by fine not less than five dollars, nor more than five hundred dollars, or by imprisonment for a period not to exceed one year, or by both such fine and imprisonment, in the discretion of the Court.

Penalty for keeping gaming house.

SEC. 2. Any person or persons keeping the building, instruments, or means for said gaming, shall be punished by the same fine or imprisonment, or by both, as is prescribed in the preceding section.

Implements for gaming to be destroyed by Marshal.

SEC. 3. Any instrument kept for the purpose of gaming for money, shall, upon conviction of the person or persons keeping the same, as is prescribed in the preceding section, be destroyed by the Marshal of the city of Detroit, under the order of the Recorder of said city: and if the said Marshal shall refuse or neglect to obey such order, or if he returns to the owner any instrument ordered to be destroyed, or uses, sells, or in any other manner disposes of the same, save in accordance with the said order, he shall be fined two hundred and fifty dollars for each and every offence.

Recorder's Court to issue warrant on complained of suspicion.

SEC. 4. If any person shall make complaint before the Recorder's Court of said city, that he suspects, or has probable cause to suspect, that any house or other building is used for the purpose of gaming for money, and that persons resort to the same for the purpose of gaming therein, the said Court shall issue a warrant, commanding the Marshal, or any Assistant Marshal, of said city, to enter into such house or building, and there to arrest all persons who shall be there found playing for money, and also the keepers of said house or building, and to take into their custody all the instruments of gaming there found, and to bring said persons and instruments before said Court, to be dealt with according to law.

CHAPTER LXVII.

To Prohibit and Prevent Fraudulent Games, Practices and Devices.

SECTION 1. Any person who shall manage, use or practice, or who shall attempt to manage, use or practice, or who shall aid in the management, use or practice of any kind of fraudulent game, device or practice within said city, with the intent to cheat or defraud another, shall, upon conviction thereof, be punished by a fine not to exceed five hundred dollars, or by imprisonment not to exceed two years, or by both said fine and imprisonment, in the discretion of the Court. Punishment for fraudulent games, practices, &c.

SEC. 2. Whenever any person shall be convicted under the preceding section, three different times for separate offences, he shall, for the third offence, receive the extreme punishment provided in said section. Punishment on third conviction.

SEC. 3. Any person convicted under this ordinance may, in addition to the punishment herein prescribed, be ordered by the Court to enter into a recognizance, with at least one surety, for his good behavior for a period not to exceed one year, and in default thereof may be committed to the county jail of Wayne county, or to any jail, prison, work house or house of correction of said city, there to remain until he shall find said surety, or until he is discharged by due course of law. Persons convicted may be required to give security.

CHAPTER LXVIII.

Relative to Shows, Theatrical Entertainments, &c.

SECTION 1. Chapter sixty-one of the Revised Ordinances of 1855 is hereby amended so as to read as follows: Sec. 1. It shall not be lawful for any person or persons to make or exhibit any show or shows, or to perform any play or plays, games, theatrical or other performances or exhibitions whatsoever, or to exhibit any natural or other curiosities for which pay or compensation of any kind shall be required, demanded or received, without having previously been licensed so to do, by the authority of the Common Council of the city of Detroit; and any person or persons offending against the provisions of this ordinance shall be liable to a fine of not exceeding two hun- Showmen to be licensed. Penalty for neglect of.

TITLE XI. CHAPTER 68.

Marshal or his deputy to arrest offenders.

dred dollars for every offence. The Marshal or Deputy Marshal is hereby authorized, and it is made his duty, in any case wherein the provisions of this chapter shall be violated, or not complied with, to arrest the person or persons offending against the same, and bring him or them before the Mayor, Recorder or any Alderman of said city, who is hereby authorized and directed to hold such person or persons to bail for his or their appearance at the next ensuing term of the Recorder's Court, to answer any alleged offence in such case: *Provided*, Any such person may be discharged by the Mayor, Recorder or President of the Common Council, upon paying such sum as may be directed in such case to be paid by the Committee on Licenses of the Common Council, and costs.

Proviso.

Persons wishing to obtain license to apply to City Clerk.

SEC. 2. It shall be the duty of all or every such person or persons who may be desirous of exhibiting any natural or other curiosities, or shows, or to perform any games or theatrical exhibitions, or any other games, shows or public entertainments of whatever nature, for which money, pay or any compensation whatever shall be required or received, to make application to the City Clerk for a license; and the said license may be granted by the City Clerk, whenever payment to the City Treasurer has been made of such sum as may be prescribed by the Common Council, or in the absence of any such prescription by the Common Council, such sum as may be prescribed by the Committee on Licenses of said Common Council.

SEC. 3. The City Clerk shall be entitled to ask, demand and receive the following prices for all shows, exhibitions, concerts, &c., as hereinafter mentioned, viz.:

For the first exhibition of any kind, by itinerant persons or showmen, and not hereinafter specified, - - -	$ 5 00
For each subsequent exhibition by the same person or persons and in continuation of a series, - - - - -	3 00
For each concert or musical entertainment, the charge for admission to which does not exceed fifty cents, - -	5 00
For each concert or musical entertainment, the charge for admission to which exceeds fifty cents—first exhibition, -	15 00
For each subsequent exhibition, - - - - - -	5 00
For all concerts, whether theatrical or otherwise, for which any charge for admission is made, whether ostensibly for refreshments or not, per year, - - - - - - -	50 00

For all circuses, menageries or other exhibitions performing under canvas—each exhibition, - - - - -	25 00
For all shows, usually denominated side shows—each day -	5 00
For all private concerts given in public halls, and admission fee charged, - - - - - - - - - -	10 00
For all theatres, per year, - - - - - - -	50 00

CHAPTER LXIX.

Relative to the Collection of License Moneys.

License moneys to be paid before delivery of license.

SECTION 1. It shall be the duty of the Clerk of the city of Detroit to make out all licenses which shall from time to time be granted by the Common Council, but no such license shall hereafter be issued or delivered until the sum required for the same has been fully paid to the Treasurer of the city of Detroit.

TITLE TWELVE.

OF PORTERS, RUNNERS, AND THE ARRIVAL AND DEPARTURE OF BOATS AND CARS.

CHAPTER LXX.

Relative to Licensing Porters and Runners.

Porters and runners to be licensed.

SECTION 1. The Mayor of the city of Detroit, for the time being, shall have power from time to time to issue licenses under his hand and seal, to so many and to such persons as he shall think proper, to carry on the business of public porters or runners for hotels, and all omnibus agents, omnibus drivers, and drivers of baggage, and all other persons when acting as porters or runners for hotels; and the Mayor or Recorder, or any three Aldermen of the city, shall have pewer to revoke all or any of such licenses.

TITLE XII. CHAPTER 70.

When license to expire.

SEC. 2. All such licenses shall expire on the seventh day of April next after the date thereof, and may be renewed on application of the holders thereof.

Fees for license.

SEC. 3. For every such license, shall be paid by the person applying for the same, the sum of one dollar, and for every renewal, the same sum.

Persons not to act without license.

SEC. 4. No person shall act or engage in the business of a public porter or runner for any hotel, or as an omnibus agent, omnibus driver, or driver of baggage, acting as porters or runners for hotels, without being duly licensed as such by the Mayor, under a penalty not exceeding five dollars, in the discretion of the Court, and costs of prosecution, for every such offence.

Porters and runners, &c., to wear a badge.

SEC. 5. Every public porter or runner, omnibus agent, omnibus driver and baggage driver, and all other persons acting as runners for hotels, shall wear a badge on his hat, and in a conspicuous place on his body, on which shall be legibly and plainly engraved or printed, his name and the number of his license, under a penalty not to exceed five dollars, in the discretion of the court, and the costs of prosecution, for each neglect of the provisions of this section.

Porters, runners, &c., to have a card containing his name, &c. in carriage.

SEC. 6. Every public porter or runner, omnibus agent, omnibus driver or baggage driver, and all other persons acting as porters or runners for hotels, shall have on a card or a plate, printed or engraved, his name and the number of his license, and also the prices or rates of fare allowed by law for omnibuses, hackney coaches, &c., in legible characters, which shall be nailed on a conspicuous part of his carriage, omnibus, wagon, sleigh, wheel-barrow or hand cart, under a penalty not to exceed five dollars, in the discretion of the Court, and the costs of prosecution, for every violation of the provisions of this section.

Porters and runners to execute bond.

SEC. 7. Every person to whom such licenses shall be granted, shall first execute to the city of Detroit, a bond with one or more sufficient sureties, to be approved by the Mayor, in the penalty of five hundred dollars, conditioned that he will conduct himself in a decent and orderly manner while acting as such porter, runner, omnibus agent, omnibus driver, or driver of baggage, when acting as porters or runners for hotels, and in all respects comply with the provisions of this ordinance: *Provided, however*, That it shall be lawful for such sureties or either of them, to vacate such bond by giving ten days' notice in writing to the Mayor, and in such case the said license shall be annulled and made void, unless other sureties are furnished as above provided.

Not to approach within twenty feet of boats and cars, when.

SEC. 8. No porter, runner, omnibus agent, omnibus driver, driver of baggage, or other persons acting as porters or runners for hotels, so licensed as aforesaid, shall, on the arrival of any steamboat or railroad cars in the city of Detroit, for a period of fifteen minutes thereafter, go upon or approach within twenty feet of the wharf or depot where such steamboat or railroad cars have made fast or stopped running, or are about to make fast or stop running; unless such porter, runner, omnibus agent, omnibus driver, or driver of baggage be requested by a passenger to remove some trunk or other baggage from said wharf or depot, in which case it shall be lawful to go near, in or upon such steamboat or depot for such purpose, under a penalty not to exceed five dollars, in the discretion of the Court, and costs of prosecution, for every such offence.

Punishment for acting without license.

SEC. 9. No person shall act as porter or runner, or omnibus agent, omnibus driver or baggage driver, when acting as runner or porter for any public house or hotel in the city of Detroit, without being duly licensed according to the provisions of this ordinance, under a penalty not to exceed twenty-five dollars, in the discretion of the Court, for every such offence.

When license forfeited.

SEC. 10. On conviction of any porter, runner, omnibus agent, omnibus driver, or baggage driver, or other person acting as porter or runner for any hotel or public house, licensed as aforesaid, before the Recorder's Court, of any violation of the provisions of this ordinance, the Mayor or Recorder shall, in his discretion, be authorized, in addition to the fines hereinbefore provided, to vacate and annul any such license that may then be held by any such porter, runner, omnibus agent, omnibus driver or driver of baggage, and to declare the bond of such person forfeited.

When City Attorney to put bond in suit.

SEC. 11. On the forfeiture of the bond of any such porter, runner, omnibus agent, omnibus driver, driver of baggage or other person, as provided in the preceding section, it shall be the duty of the City Attorney to prosecute the principal and sureties named in such bond for the benefit of the city.

TITLE XII.
CHAPTER 71.

CHAPTER LXXI.

Relative to the Departure and Arrival of Boats and Cars.

Carriages not to be kept within 20 feet of depot on arrival of cars.

SECTION 1. That no person shall, on the arrival of any railroad cars in said city, nor for the period of thirty minutes previously to the departure of any railroad cars from said city, have or keep any carriage, wagon, cart or other vehicle within twenty feet of the place where such railroad cars shall have ceased running, or are about to depart from said city.

Where carriages to stand on arrival and departure of steamboats.

SEC. 2. No person shall, on the arrival of any steamboat or vessel at any wharf in said city, nor for the period of thirty minutes thereafter, nor for the period of thirty minutes previously to the departure of such steamboats or vessels, have or keep any carriage, wagon, cart or other vehicle, within sixty feet of the place where such steamboat or vessel has or is about to be made fast, or depart from said city. Any person violating this or the preceding section, shall, for every violation, on conviction before the Recorder's Court, forfeit a sum not exceeding one hundred dollars and costs of prosecution.

Further regulations.

SEC. 3. All carriages, wagons, carts and other vehicles, the keepers whereof are waiting for employment from any railroad cars, steamboats or vessels, shall stand on either side of the street or alley, so as to leave the centre thereof, and access to each house thereon, open and unobstructed, for the free passage of carriages, wagons, carts and other vehicles, and foot passengers. Any person violating this section, shall, for every violation, on conviction before the Recorder's Court, forfeit a sum not exceeding fifty dollars and costs of prosecution.

Disorderly conduct at boats and cars prohibited.

SEC. 4. If any person shall, on the arrival or departure of any railroad cars, steamboats or vessels, at or from said city, or for the period of thirty minutes after the arrival or before the departure of such railroad cars, steamboats or vessels, and within sixty feet of the wharf or depot where such railroad cars, steamboats or vessels have, or are about to stop running, or being made fast, or depart from said city, make, aid, countenance or assist in making, any loud or boisterous noise, disturbance or improper diversion, or shall be guilty of any indecent, immoral or insulting conduct, language or behavior, such person shall, for every such offence, on conviction before said Recorder's Court, forfeit a sum not exceeding one hundred dollars and costs of prosecution.

False representation to strangers, punishment.

SEC. 5. If any person shall, by any false or deceitful representations to any stranger or traveler in said city, induce or prevail on such stranger or traveler to go to and put up at any hotel, tavern, grocery or other house of entertainment in said city, such person shall, for every such offence, on conviction before the Recorder's Court, forfeit a sum not exceeding one hundred dollars and costs of prosecution.

Duty of officers.

SEC. 6. It shall be the special duty of the Marshal and all the Constables of said city, to make complaint of all violations of this chapter.

Teamsters may haul freight.

SEC. 7. Nothing contained in the first and second sections of this chapter shall be construed to prevent any teamster from hauling freight to any steamboat or vessel about to depart from said city.

Propellers to be provided with spark catchers.

SEC. 8. No propeller shall be permitted to approach within fifty feet of any wharf in this city, or lie at any wharf in this city, while fired up, unless her smoke pipe shall be covered with a good and sufficient spark catcher, or other covering to prevent the emission of sparks or coals from her said pipe; and in case the captain or officers of any propeller shall permit the same to approach or lie at any wharf, contrary to the provisions of this section, he or they shall be liable to a fine not exceeding one hundred dollars, to be recovered with costs by prosecution in the Recorder's Court.

Penalty.

TITLE THIRTEEN.

OF PAUPERS.

CHAPTER LXXII.

Relative to Paupers and their Support.

Vessels not to land paupers.

SECTION 1. If any owner, captain or master of a vessel, or other person shall, by land or water, bring and leave within the limits of this city, any person or persons, poor and unable to maintain themselves, they shall forthwith, or as soon as may be thereafter, transport

TITLE XIV. CHAPTER 73.

the same back to the place whence they were taken; and shall provide all the necessary means of comfort and subsistence for such paupers, if requested by them or by any citizen, until so transported.

Persons bringing paupers to support them.

SEC. 2. In case of refusal or neglect to provide for such paupers the necessary means of comfort and subsistence according to the foregoing section, and any member of the Common Council, or Director of the Poor, shall make such provision, the same may be recovered back, and may form part of the judgment in a prosecution for a violation of this chapter.

Penalty.

SEC. 3. Any violation of the two preceding sections of this chapter, may be punished with a fine not exceeding fifty dollars and costs of prosecution.

Director of poor, his duties.

SEC. 4. The Director of the Poor for said city, shall have and exercise the same powers and duties, and be subject to the same liabilities and restrictions as the laws of this State prescribe relative to Directors of the Poor in any township of this State; and the laws of this State relative to township and county paupers shall be observed with respect to such paupers in said city; and all suits and prosecutions for violations of such laws, may be brought in the Recorder's Court of said city.

TITLE FOURTEEN.

MISCELLANEOUS.

CHAPTER LXXIII.

Relative to Cancelling the Orders, Warrants and Due Bills of the City of Detroit.

Treasurer to cancel warrants, &c.

SECTION 1. That the City Treasurer shall, without delay, procure a proper cancelling hammer, such as is ordinarily used by banking institutions, with which he shall immediately cut, mark and cancel every order, due bill, warrant or other evidence of debt, issued by the city of Detroit, or by the Common Council of said city, or under their direction, which now are in the City Treasury; and hereafter the said Treasurer shall, as soon as any order, due bill, or warrant, or other evidence of debt heretofore issued, or which hereafter shall or may at any time or times be issued by said city of Detroit, or by said Common Council, or by or under their direction or authority, shall come or be paid into the Treasury of said city, cut, mark and cancel the same with said cancelling hammer.

To keep cancelled warrants.

SEC. 2. After the City Treasurer shall have so cut, marked and cancelled said orders, warrants, due bills or other evidences of debt, as aforesaid, he shall carefully and safely file and keep the same until the further order or action of said Common Council.

To record the same.

SEC. 3. It shall be the duty of the City Treasurer, from and after the passage of this chapter, to keep a book or record, in which he shall enter as soon as he receives the same, the number, date and amount of each and every warrant, order, due bill and evidence of debt, as aforesaid, received into the City Treasury; and whenever the City Treasurer shall report to said Common Council any amount of warrants, orders, due bills or other evidences of debt, as hereinafter provided for, he shall accompany his report with a schedule or list of said warrants, orders, due bills or other evidences of debt so reported, with the number, date and amount of each.

Warrants, &c., to be returned to Council and destroyed.

SEC. 4. Whenever the City Treasurer shall have in his possession one thousand dollars of cut, marked and cancelled warrants, orders, due bills or other evidences of debt, issued or hereafter to be issued, as aforesaid, he shall report the fact to the said Common Council, whilst in session, and thereupon, at the same session of said Council, or at the next regular meeting, said Council shall cause said orders, due bills, warrants or other evidences of debt aforesaid, to be carefully examined and checked on the warrant book, in presence of the Council, by a committee of three, to be appointed from time to time by the Mayor, of whom the Clerk shall be one, and the same having been so counted, examined and checked, shall be forthwith burned, or otherwise destroyed, in the presence of the Council, and the amount so destroyed, with the number or other suitable designation of each, shall be entered on the journal of the Council.

TITLE XIV.
CHAPTER 74.

CHAPTER LXXIV.

To Prescribe and Regulate the Speed of Cars and Exgines on Railroads within the limits of the City.

Not to exceed 6 miles per hour.

SECTION 1. That the rate of speed of engines and cars on railroads within the limits of the city shall not exceed six miles per hour, and any engineer, driver or conductor having charge of an engine, car or train of cars upon any railroad in said city, who shall suffer or cause said engine, car or train of cars to go over said railroad, within said city, at a greater rate of speed than six miles an hour, shall be punished by a fine of not less than twenty-five dollars, nor more than one hundred dollars, or by imprisonment not to exceed six months, or by both said fine and imprisonment, in the discretion of the Court.

SEC. 2. This ordinance shall take effect and be in force five days after its passage.

CHAPTER LXXV.

Relative to the Powers and Duties of the Assessor and his Assistants.

Assessor to give bonds.

SECTION 1. The Assessor of said city shall keep his office in such place as shall be designated and provided by the Common Council, and shall give bonds to the city, with sufficient sureties, in the sum of twenty thousand dollars.

Assistant Assessor to be under the control of Assessor, compensat'n.

SEC. 2. The Assistant Assessors shall be subordinate to the Assessor, and in all respects subject to his direction. Their compensation shall be three dollars per day each, and shall be paid on the certificate of the Assessor, setting forth the actual number of days they have been employed in the business of the city.

Assessor to furnish to City Clerk a list of stationery required by him.

SEC. 3. The Assessor shall, at the end of each and every year, report to the City Clerk a list of all books, stationery and printing which will be required in his office during the ensuing year; and shall have power to procure of the contractor for supplying stationery, books or printing to the city, such books, stationery and printing as he may from time to time require; and all bills for stationery, books or printing, thus procured, shall be certified by him, and, upon their presentation, thus certified, the Controller shall draw his warrant therefor.

SEC. 4. The Assessor shall keep in his office a book of accounts of all the expenses in his office, and shall report to the Common Council on the first Tuesday of January in each year, a full and particular statement of said expenses. Assessor to keep account of expenses of his office.

SEC. 5. He shall keep in his office complete sets of all assessment rolls made by him and confirmed by the Common Council, and said assessment rolls, together with all books belonging to the office, and containing any assessment of property, shall be open to inspection in his office by any tax payer of the city. To keep assessment rolls in his office, rolls to be open to inspection of tax payers.

SEC. 6. He may, whenever it is necessary, require the services of the City Surveyor to aid him in ascertaining the dimensions and boundaries of any real estate within the city. City Surveyor to assist him in certain cases.

SEC. 7. It shall be the duty of the Assessor, when directed by the Controller, to prepare the tax rolls for highway, sewer, school and city taxes of each ward in said city, and when said rolls are completed, the same shall be delivered to the City Treasurer, as provided by law, and the said Assessor shall file and keep in his office all opinions given him by the City Attorney. To complete rolls when directed by Controller. To file opinions given by City Attor'y.

CHAPTER LXXVI.

Relative to the Disposition of Lands bid in by the City for Taxes or Assessments.

SECTION 1. Whenever any lands, bid in for the city under the provisions of section twenty-one of chapter ninth of the revised charter of said city, of the year 1857, shall not be redeemed by the owner or other persons interested in said lands, within one year from the day on which said lands are so bid in, it shall be lawful for the City Treasurer, and he hereby is authorized, to sell, assign and transfer to any person or persons who shall pay the tax or assessment, together with the costs and charges for which said land was sold, all the interest which the city has acquired in said land by reason of said bid. And he shall give to the person or persons who shall so pay said tax Treasurer may dispose of lands bid in by city in certain cases.

TITLE XIV. CHAPTER 77.

Treasurer to give certificate of such sale.

or assessment, together with said costs and charges, a certificate of the fact of such payment, in which certificate the land or lands for which such payment is made shall be particularly described.

Controller to make transfer on presentation of such certificate.

SEC. 2. Upon presentation to him of the certificate provided for in the foregoing section, the City Controller shall, under the seal of the city, execute to the person named in the certificate a full and absolute assignment and transfer of the conveyance or certificate of sale of the land or lands for which the person or persons named in said certificate of the Treasurer shall have made said payment.

Treasurer to report the fact of purchasers failing to make good their bids, to the Council.

SEC. 3. It shall be the duty of the City Treasurer, whenever persons bidding for lands at any sale for delinquent taxes or assessments, shall fail to pay the amount of their said bid, to report the fact to the Common Council.

CHAPTER LXXVII.

To Provide for the keeping a Record of Lots and parts of Lots, subject to Assessment for Drainage.

City Assessor to place on assessment rolls yearly all lots drained into private sewers, &c.

SECTION 1. That it is made the duty of the City Assessor, once in each year, to ascertain and place upon the assessment rolls all lots, premises or subdivisions thereof drained by private sewers, or drains leading into or connected with any public sewer or drain; and he shall designate on said rolls every lot, premises or subdivisions thereof, on which there is a cellar, and every lot, premises or subdivisions thereof, drained as aforesaid, on which there is no cellar; and also every lot, premises or subdivision thereof on which there is any hotel, tavern, tannery, or any kind of manufactory.

CHAPTER LXXVIII.

To Define the Powers and Duties of the Marshal and his Assistants.

Marshal to be chief of police.

SECTION 1. The City Marshal shall be Chief of the Police of the city of Detroit, and all Constables, Policemen, Watchmen and Assistant Marshals, when acting under the ordinances of the city, or the orders and resolutions of the Common Council, shall be subordinate to him.

To receive and be responsible for all writs, process, &c.

SEC. 2. He shall receive and be responsible for the execution of all writs, process, orders, resolutions and proceedings of any nature, which may be directed to the Marshal, his Assistants, or to any Constable, Policeman or Watchman of the city, under the ordinances of the city, or emanating from the Common Council, and shall report to the Mayor all officers in his department who fail to do their duty.

To keep a register of all papers served by him, &c.; to receive from City Clerk and file certified copies of all orders.

SEC. 3. He shall keep in a book, to be provided for the purpose, a list of all process, writs, notices and papers of every kind served by him or his subordinates, and shall receive from the City Clerk, and file in his office, certified copies of every order or resolution of the Common Council, under which he or they may be required to do any act, and shall file and keep in his office every opinion given to him by the City Attorney.

To appoint paid officers to attend sittings of Council.

SEC. 4. He shall, from time to time, appoint one or more of his Assistants, or any paid Constable, Policeman or Watchman, to attend the meetings of the Common Council: *Provided*, That he shall appoint no officer to perform that duty who is not in the receipt of a regular compensation from the city.

To receive orders from Mayor relative to police.

SEC. 5. He shall receive and be the medium of all the lawful orders of the Mayor, relating to the Police, or requiring the services of any of his subordinates, and shall possess the immediate control of the operations of the Police.

To see that all ordinances are enforced.

SEC. 6. He shall aid in the suppression of all crime and detection of all offenders within the limits of the city, and shall see that all ordinances of the city shall be strictly enforced.

To wear a badge marked "Police."

SEC. 7. He and his Assistants, and all Constables, Officers, Police and Watchmen of the city shall wear a metallic badge in some conspicuous place upon their persons, on which shall be marked, in legible characters, the word "Police."

To deliver all official papers entrusted to him.

SEC. 8. He shall serve all papers and notices of every kind relating to the business of the city, and delivered to him by the Mayor, Common Council, Controller, City Attorney, City Clerk, City Treasurer, and Committees of the Council.

Clerks of Market ex-officio Deputy Marshals.

SEC. 9. For the purpose of enforcing the Police regulations relative to the public markets, the Clerks of Markets within the city are hereby made ex-officio Assistant Marshals for that purpose, and shall,

TITLE XIV. CHAPTER 79.

under the direction of the Marshal, have power to arrest all persons offending against said regulations: *Provided*, That said Clerks shall receive no fees or compensations for services rendered under this section, and that they shall have no other or further power than to arrest in the cases herein specified.

Proviso.

Marshal to notify Aldermen of special meetings.

SEC. 10. The Marshal shall notify Aldermen of all special meetings of the Common Council, and shall deliver to officers of the city all resolutions, papers and proceedings which shall be delivered to him for that purpose by the City Clerk.

May direct his subordinates to perform his duties.

SEC. 11. He shall have power to direct his Assistants and all subordinate officers, who are paid out of the City Treasury, to perform any of the duties which are herein devolved upon him.

To give bonds and account to Controller quarterly.

SEC. 12. He shall give bonds to the city in the sum of two thousand dollars, and shall, at the end of every quarter, account under oath to the City Controller, for all moneys which have passed through his hands and belong to the city, save fines, penalties and fees collected in the Courts.

To make annual report.

SEC. 13. He shall, on the first Tuesday of January in each year, report in writing, to the Common Council, the number of subordinates who have acted in his office during the year, the nature of their duties, and the amount of compensation; also, the general operations of his office during the year, and such other matters as he deems proper.

To visit police stations semi-weekly.

SEC. 14. He shall, in addition to the above powers and duties, visit, at least twice in each week, each and every station or place where any Policeman or other officer of the city is stationed, and see that said Policeman or other officer is faithful and diligent in the performance of his duty; and if he shall find any such Policeman or officer absent from his place or station, without proper excuse, he shall report the same to the Mayor.

CHAPTER LXXIX.

Relative to Weights and Measures.

SECTION 1. That the provisions of chapter thirty-one of the Revised Statutes of the State of Michigan, of the year 1846, relative to Township Clerks, shall be, and hereby are, made applicable to the Sealer of Weights and Measures in and for said city of Detroit, and the said Sealer of Weights and Measures shall perform the same duties, at the same time, and in the same manner, and receive the same compensation therefor, as are enjoined and permitted in said chapter upon and to said Township Clerks.

Chap. 31 R. S. made applicable to Sealer of Weights and Measures in Detroit.

SEC. 2. Any person who shall resist the Sealer of Weights and Measures in the performance of his duty, either by refusing him admittance to the house, store or other place where the weights, scales, beams and measures of said person are kept, or may be, or by refusing to produce, or secreting said weights, scales, beams and measures, or by assaulting or in any manner preventing said Sealer of Weights and Measures, shall be punished by a fine of not more than one hundred dollars, or by imprisonment not to exceed ninety days.

Penalty for resisting Sealer of Weights and Measures.

SEC. 3. Any person who shall, for the purpose of buying and selling, use beams, scales, weights or measures which are not in accordance with the standard fixed by law, having knowledge of the same, shall, upon conviction thereof, be punished for the first offence by a fine of ten dollars or ten days' imprisonment, and for each subsequent offence by a fine of fifty dollars or by thirty days' imprisonment, or by both, in the discretion of the Court.

Penalty for using false weights and measures, &c.

CHAPTER LXXX.

Relative to the Imprisonment of Offenders.

SECTION 1. That whenever, by the terms of any ordinance of said city, it is provided that any person convicted of an offence shall be imprisoned, said person may be confined either in the county jail of the county of Wayne, or in any jail, workhouse, house of correction or alms house of said city, in the discretion of the Court.

Powers of Court relative to persons convicted under the city ordinances.

TITLE XIV.
CHAPTER 81.

CHAPTER LXXXI.

To Prescribe and Define the Duties of Standing Committees.

SECTION 1. That the following shall be the duties of Standing Committees of the said Common Council, to wit:

Committee on Claims to examine all accounts.

1. The Committee on Claims shall examine into and report upon all matters of account or claim, either in favor of or against said city.

Committee on Ways and Means to report and examine into all matters of finance.

2. The Committee on Ways and Means shall examine into and report upon all such matters relative to the revenue of the city, as shall be referred to them; they shall inquire into the state of the city debt, the revenue, and the expenditures of the city; and whether any or what retrenchment can be made with advantage; and shall report, from time to time, such provisions and arrangements as may be promotive of order, economy and accountability in the conduct of the fiscal concerns of the city. They shall examine into and report upon the efficiency of all official bonds, and all such matters not constituting a claim against the city, as shall be referred to them, and shall, with the City Controller, make and report the estimates for the yearly expenditures.

Committee on Streets all matters relative to walks, &c., &c.

3. The Committee on Streets shall examine into and report upon all such matters as may be referred to them relative to streets, alleys and sidewalks within the city, and shall, at the end of each year, report to the Common Council what improvements of any nature will be needed upon the streets, alleys and sidewalks of the city, during the ensuing year, and an estimate of the expense of the same.

Health all matters relative to public health.

4. The Committee on Health shall examine into and report upon all matters relating to or in any way affecting the public health, which shall be referred to them; and it shall be their duty to report, from time to time, to the Common Council, such plans and suggestions relative to the cleanliness and health of the city, as they may deem proper.

Fire Dep't all matters relative thereto.

5. The Committee on Fire Department shall examine into and report upon all matters connected with the Fire Department of the city and the suppression of fires, which may be referred to them, and shall, at the end of each year, report to the Common Council an estimate of all the expenses which will be necessary for the operation of the Fire Department of the city during the ensuing year.

6. The Committee on Hydraulics shall examine into and report upon the condition of the Hydraulics of the city, whenever so directed by the Common Council; and to them shall be referred all reports and communications from the Board of Commissioners of the Water Works.

Hydraulics all matters relative to water works.

7. The Committee on Markets shall examine into and report upon all matters connected with the public markets, which may be referred to them.

Markets all matters relative to public markets.

8. The Committee on Taxes shall examine into and report upon all questions brought before the Common Council concerning taxes, which may be referred to them.

Taxes matters relative to taxation.

9. The Committee on Printing shall examine into and report upon all matters connected with the city printing, which may be referred to them. They shall also, at the end of the year, report to the Common Council an estimate of the expense necessary for the city printing in the ensuing year.

Printing, matters relative thereto.

10. The Committee on Gas Lights shall report upon all matters connected with the lighting of the city, which may be referred to them. To them shall be referred all reports of the Gas Company; and they shall, at the end of each year, report to the Common Council the number, location and cost of lights which will be necessary in the ensuing year.

Gas Lights, all things relative to street lamps, &c.

11. The Committee on Public Buildings shall examine into and report upon the condition of all buildings belonging to the city; all questions and plans for repairs, erection and construction of public buildings, shall be referred to them; and they shall, at the end of each year, report to the Common Council the estimated expenses of their department for the ensuing year.

Public Buildings, relative to all buildings owned by city.

12. The Committee on Parks shall examine into and report upon the condition of all public parks; upon the improvements, adornment and protection thereof; and shall, at the end of each year, report the estimated expenses of their department during the ensuing year.

Parks, relative to same.

13. The Committee on Sewers shall examine into and report upon all questions connected with the construction of sewers which may be referred to them.

Sewers, to examine all matters relative to same.

14. The Committee on Licenses shall examine into and report upon all questions connected with licenses, which may be referred to them.

Licenses, all matters relative to licenses.

TITLE XIV: CHAPTER 82.

Committees may require the services of any officer.

SEC. 2. Every committee, in the discharge of their duty, may require the services of any officer of the city, whose duties are in any manner connected with the subject under investigation by the committee.

Committees not to make contracts.

SEC. 3. No committee shall exercise any executive functions, nor perform any duty save that usual to legislative bodies; nor shall they in any case order the doing of any work, or the cessation thereof, enter into any contract, or change or vary one already made; and any act performed by them, which is unauthorized by this ordinance, shall be null and void.

Matters to be referred to the appropriate committee.

SEC. 4. The Common Council shall always refer matters to the appropriate committee; nor shall any matter be referred to a committee which does not directly relate to the department which that committee has been appointed to.

CHAPTER LXXXII.

Relative to the taking of Testimony before Committees.

Chairman of any committee may issue subpœnas and compel the attendance of witnesses.

SECTION 1. That the presiding officer of any board, or the chairman of any committee of the Common Council, who are engaged in the consideration, or to whom have been referred the investigation of any claim for damages, money or recompense against said board, or against the city, may issue subpœnas under their hands, and sealed with the corporate seal of said city, directed to any person whom said board or committee deem necessary as a witness in any matter pending before them, and ordering said person to appear before said committee or board at such time and place, and to testify concerning such matter or thing, as in said subpœna shall be designated.

May issue attachment.

SEC. 2. If the person so subpœnaed shall fail to appear at said time and place, an attachment shall be issued to compel his appearance, which attachment shall be signed and sealed, as is provided for subpœnas in the preceding section.

Party making claim to be heard.

SEC. 3. The person or party making such claim shall be entitled to a hearing before said board or committee, and to process to compel the appearance of witnesses in his behalf.

SEC. 4. The Marshal or Assistant Marshals of said city shall serve all process issuing under this ordinance. Said process shall be served in the manner like processes are served in courts of Justices of the Peace, and shall be returned to the presiding officer or chairman issuing them: *Provided, always*, That in case of the absence of the chairman of any committee, the person whose name appears next to his in the order of appointment of said committee, shall act as chairman, and may issue all process herein provided for.

Marshal or deputy to serve process.

SEC. 5. The statements of all persons concerning any such claim, made before any board or committee, as herein provided, shall, in all cases, be taken under oath, and reduced to writing by the chairman of said committee, or the presiding officer of said board, and signed by the person making the same, which statement, so signed, shall be returned by the chairman of said committee to the City Attorney, who shall file and preserve the same in his office, subject to the order of the Common Council.

Statement of parties to be under oath.

CHAPTER LXXXIII.

Extending the Limits of the Third Ward.

SECTION 1. That the limits of the Third Ward of said city shall be, and hereby are extended to Gratiot street, by adding to said Third Ward, and incorporating as part of the same all that portion of the Sixth Ward in said city bounded as follows, to wit: On the south by Croghan street, on the west by Randolph street, on the north by Gratiot street, and on the east by St. Antoine street, and by a line on the course of St. Antoine street, if extended from Clinton street to Gratiot street.

Boundaries.

SEC. 2. Nothing in this ordinance contained shall be construed to affect the basis of taxation in the Sixth or in the Third Ward, aforesaid, during the present year, or to affect or remove from office any officer continued in office by the Revised Charter of the present year, during the time for which said person is so continued in office.

CHAPTER LXXXIV.

Relative to Sidewalks on Jefferson and Woodward Avenues, and Griswold Street, from Atwater Street to Michigan Avenue.

Sikewalks on Jefferson Av. and other streets to be flagged.

SECTION 1. That hereafter, all sidewalks laid down on Jefferson avenue, between Third street and Beaubien street, in said city; on Woodward avenue, between Grand River street and the Detroit river, in said city; and on Griswold street, from Atwater street to Michigan avenue, in said city, shall be constructed of stone flagging, and of no other material.

Dimensions of flags to be used.

SEC. 2. The flags used in the construction of said sidewalks shall be at least forty-eight inches in length, twenty-four inches in width, and four inches thick.

Expenses, how defrayed

SEC. 4. The expense of constructing said sidewalks shall be defrayed in the same manner in which the expense of constructing plank sidewalks is now defrayed; and all ordinances and parts of ordinances relative to the manner of constructing and of making assessments for the construction of sidewalks are hereby made part of this ordinance, except so far as they relate to the material of which said sidewalks shall be constructed.

CHAPTER LXXXV.

To Regulate the Width of Sidewalks on Wayne Street.

Width of sidewalks on Wayne st., (portion of.)

SECTION 1. That the sidewalks on both sides of Wayne street, in said city of Detroit, shall, and hereby are directed to be made and maintained the width of twelve feet, from Fort street to Michigan avenue.

CHAPTER LXXXVI.

Relative to the Sale of Cattle in the City of Detroit.

No cattle to be offered for sale in sts.

SECTION 1. It shall not be lawful for any person or persons to sell or offer for public sale any horse or neat cattle, sheep or hogs, in any of the streets, lanes or alleys of said city, lying at a greater distance than three hundred feet from one or the other of the public wood yards; and any person or persons who shall expose or offer for sale any horse or neat cattle in any street, lane or alley without or beyond said limits, shall, for each offence, upon conviction thereof, pay a fine of five dollars and costs of prosecution.

Penalty.

SEC. 2. The Clerk of the Hay Scales shall have the right to designate the place where horses or neat cattle may be exposed for sale; and the Clerks of both Hay Markets aforesaid are hereby clothed with the power of Assistant Marshals, for the purpose of enforcing this ordinance and all other ordinances relative to the sale of cattle in said city.

Clerks of hay scales to designate place where cattle, &c., be sold.

SEC. 3. The Clerks of said Hay Scales shall be entitled to demand and receive from the owners or parties in charge of horses or neat cattle offered or exposed for sale as aforesaid, ten cents for each and every horse and head of neat cattle so offered or exposed for sale, which sums, with costs of prosecution, may be recovered before the Recorder's Court.

What sum clerks may ask and receive from persons in charge of cattle.

SEC. 4. The Clerks of said Hay Scales shall keep a just and true account of all moneys received by them by virtue of section three, and shall render said account to the Treasurer of said city, at least once in each month, and pay over to said Treasurer one-half of the whole amount of said receipts, and the remaining half the said Clerks shall be entitled to retain for their services in the premises.

Clerks to keep an account of receipts and account for same.

SEC. 5. Hereafter, no person offering or exposing for sale, within said city, a cow having a sucking calf, shall muzzle said calf, or in any manner prevent said calf, when so offered or exposed for sale, from taking its natural nutriment from its mother; and any person violating the provisions of this section shall be punished by a fine not exceeding one hundred dollars, or by imprisonment not exceeding six months.

Sucking calves not to be muzzled.

AN ORDINANCE to give effect to the Compiled Ordinance of eighteen hundred and fifty-nine.

It is hereby ordained by the Common Council of the City of Detroit,

SEC. 1. That the edition of the Ordinances of the City of Detroit, compiled and published under the direction of the City Clerk agreeable to and in accordance with the report of the Committee on claims and accounts, adopted May 31, 1859, unanimously shall be called "The Compiled Ordinance of the City of Detroit for the year 1859," and the same, together with this Ordinance, shall take effect and go into operation from and after the first day of October, A. D., 1859.

SEC. 2. All by-laws and ordinances, or parts of by-laws and ordinances, repugnant to, or in any manner inconsistent with, the edition of Ordinances so arranged and published by the said City Clerk as aforesaid, shall be repealed from and after the taking effect of the said compiled ordinances arranged and published by said City Clerk.

SEC. 3. The repeal provided for in the preceding section, shall not affect any act done, or any right accruing or accrued, or established, or any suit had or commenced for any purpose whatever, before the time when such repeal shall take effect; nor shall any offence committed, or penalty or forfeiture incurred, under any of the ordinance or by-laws repealed by the preceding section, and before the time when such repeal shall take effect, be affected by such repeal.

SEC. 4. No suit or prosecution, pending at the time of the said repeal, for any offence committed, or for the recovery of any penalty or forfeiture incurred, under any of the ordinances or by-laws repealed as provided for in section three, shall be affected by such repeal, except that the proceedings in such suit or prosecution shall be conformed, when necessary, to the provisions of said compiled ordinances.

SEC. 5. All persons who, at the time when the said repeal shall take effect, shall hold any office under any of the ordinances or by-laws so as aforesaid repealed, shall continue to hold the same according to the tenure thereof.

SEC. 6. No ordinance or by-law, which has heretofore been repealed, shall be revived by the repeal provided for in section three.

SEC. 7. Whenever an ordinance or by-law, or any part thereof, shall be repealed by a subsequent ordinance or by-law, such ordinance or by-law, or any part thereof, so repealed, shall not be revived by the repeal of such subsequent repealing ordinance or by-law.

SEC. 8. All ordinances and by-laws hereafter to be passed by the Common Council shall be promulgated by being printed in such manner as the Common Council shall direct; and every ordinance or by-law which does not expressly provide the time when it shall go into operation, shall take effect on the fifth day after the same has been passed.

SEC. 9. This ordinance shall take effect and be in force from and after the first day of October, A. D. 1859.

Ordained and dated in Common Council the first day of October, 1859.

JOHN PATTON, *Mayor*.

Attest: FRANCIS W. HUGHES, *City Clerk*.

At a session of the Common Council of the city of Detroit, held on the thirty-first day of May, 1859, the following report of the Committee on Claims and Accounts was unanimously adopted:

Report.—As the compilation of the ordinances for the last *two years* does not meet the necessities of the case, that the City Clerk be authorized to procure the revision, compilation, indexing, and printing of all the existing ordinances, and binding of the same in a suitable form, subject to the approval of the Council.

JOHN PATTON, *Mayor*.

Attest: FRANCIS W. HUGHES, *City Clerk*.

INDEX.

A.

B.

C.

D.

F.

G.

H.

I.

J.

L.

M.

N.

O.

P.

R.

S.

T.

W.

www.ingramcontent.com/pod-product-compliance
Lightning Source LLC
LaVergne TN
LVHW011235110826
845150LV00006B/1640